WY**PLAY HOUSE**

Hijra
By Ash Kotak

Director **Ian Brown**
Designer **Belinda Ackermann**
Lighting Designer **Tim Skelly**
Sound Designer **Mic Pool**
Movement Director **Faroque Khan**
Assistant Director **Chris Yandell**
Deputy Stage Manager **Sarah Northcott**

First performance of this production:
Courtyard Theatre, West Yorkshire Playhouse,
Saturday 9 February 2002

West Yorkshire Playhouse,
Quarry Hill,
Leeds, LS2 7UP
www.wyp.org.uk

Tickets and information 0113 213 7700

This production is supported by the Friends of the Playhouse

Yorkshire Arts

The Company
in order of appearance

Sheila	**Mala Ghedia**
Indira	**Harvey Virdi**
Madhu	**Josephine Welcome**
Aunt/Announcer/Mrs Patel	**Charubala Chokshi**
Nils	**Guy Rhys**
Guru	**Harmage Singh Kalirai**
Hijra/Bobby	**Rez Kempton**
Raj/Rani	**Raj Ghatak**

THERE WILL BE ONE INTERVAL OF TWENTY MINUTES

BSL Interpreted performance: Wednesday 27 February 7.45pm
BSL Interpreter: **Alan Haythornthwaite**
Audio Described performances: Thursday 21 February 7.45pm, Thursday
28 February 2.30pm and Tuesday 5 March 7.45pm
Audio Describers: **Jo Davy** and **Doreen Newlyn**

Smoking in the auditorium is not permitted. Please ensure that mobile
phones, pagers and digital alarm watches are SWITCHED OFF before
you enter the auditorium.

Company

Charubala Chokshi Aunt/Announcer/Mrs Patel

Before coming to Britain in the 1960's, Charubala worked with the Indian National Theatre in Bombay, winning awards from Maharashtra State and from Gujarat State in 1961.

Theatre credits include: **Kirti Sona and Ba** (Leicester Haymarket); **Untouchable** (Riverside Studios); **House of the Sun** (Theatre Royal Stratford East); **A Shaft of Sunlight** (Birmingham Repertory Theatre); and **Hijra** (Theatre Royal Plymouth and The Bush).

Television credits include: **Casualty, Gems, The Bill, Angels, Between the Lines, Dear Manju, You and Me, Love Match, Pravia's Wedding, Lake of Darkness, Specials, Porterhouse Blue, Story Store** and **Medics.**

Film credits include: **A Fish Called Wanda, My Beautiful Laundrette, Gandhi** and **Splitting Heirs.**

Radio credits include: **Citizens, Women of the Dust, Lizpeth, Beyond the Pale, Pankhiraj, House of the Sun, Untouchable, The Tiger** and **Girlies** (Radio 4); and **Pravina's Wedding** (Capital Radio).

Raj Ghatak Raj/Rani

Raj trained for a BA (hons) in English and Drama at the Central School of Speech and Drama and Queen Mary University (University of London). Upon graduating, Raj was chosen to represent the UK at a world drama festival in Jerusalem, where he premiered a monologue for one and a half hours.

Theatre credits include: **Hijra** (Theatre Royal Plymouth and The Bush); **My Dad's Corner Shop** (Birmingham Repertory and national tour); **Airport 2000** (Greenwich Theatre); **West Side Story** (Prince of Wales Theatre, West End); **Bollywood or Bust** and **Don't Look at my Sister...Innit!** (Watermans Arts Centre & national tour); **East is East** (Oldham Coliseum); and **Arrange That Marriage** (Bloomsbury Theatre and national tour).

Television and Film credits include: **Hard Cash** and **In No Time** (BBC); **Out of Sight** (Carlton); **The Escort** (Pathe Productions); **Birthday Girl** (Portobello Pictures/Miramax); **Sari & Trainers** (Stretch Limo Productions); and the forthcoming feature film **Never Say Never Mind.**

Mala Ghedia Sheila

Mala graduated from the Webber Douglas Academy of Dramatic Art in 2000.

Theatre credits include: **14 Songs, 2 Weddings & A Funeral** (National tour); **Andromache** and work for the Australian Theatre for Young People.

Whilst studying at the Webber Douglas Academy her credits included: **Live Like Pigs; David Copperfield; The Happy Journey; Lie of the Mind** and **Absolute Hell.**

Television credits include: **Home & Away** and **MTN News.**

Harmage Singh Kalirai Guru

Harmage trained at the Rose Bruford College and Ecole Jacques Lecoq.

Theatre credits include: **Behsharam** (Soho Theatre/Birmingham Repertory Theatre); **Arabian Nights** (Young Vic and national tour); **Bravely Fought the Queen** (Border Crossing); **Riddley Walker** and **The Moonstone** (Royal Exchange, Manchester); **My Beautiful Laundrette** (The Sherman, Cardiff); **Dick Whittington** (Wolverhampton Grand); **The Illusion** (The Old Vic); **Passage to India** (The Redgrave, Farnham); **Doolaly Days** (Leicester Haymarket); **Vigilantes** and **The Bhangra Dancer** (Asian Co-operative Theatre). He has also toured with Bristol Express, 7:84 Scotland, Tara Arts, Moving Parts and Tricycle Theatre Company.

His many television credits include: **Trial and Retribution** (La Plante Productions); **Fat Friends** and **A Touch of Frost** (Yorkshire TV); **Stan The Man** and **Medics** (Granada); **The Cops** (World/BBC); ; TV); **Hearts & Minds** and **Lovejoy** (Witzend); **The Knock** (Bronson Knight); **The Bill** (Thames); **Family Pride** (Central); and **The Good Guys** (LWT).

Film credits include: **Guru in Seven** (Balhar); **Brothers in Trouble** (Renegade); **Paper Mask** (Granada); **Partition** (Bandung/Channel 4); and **A Very British Coup** (Skreba).

Rez Kempton Hijra/Bobby

Trained at the Rose Bruford College of Speech and Drama.

Theatre credits include: **The Arbor** (Crucible Theatre); **Hijra** (Theatre Royal Plymouth & The Bush); **Nativity** (Birmingham Repertory Theatre) **Playboy of the Asian World** (Leicester Haymarket); **Arrange That Marriage** (Tour); **Don't Look at my Sister...Innit!** and **Private Lives** (Waterman's Art Centre); **Routes: A Journey of a Lifetime** (Europe and UK tour); **Heer Ranjha** (MAC); **Dear Elena Sergeevna** (BAC); **Games in the Backyard** (Grange Court Theatre); **Love of the Nightingale** (Tour); **The Simple Past** (The Gate); and **Twelfth Night** (Millfield Theatre Company).

Television credits include: **Lee Evans - So What Now?, Trial by Jury** and **Roger, Roger** (BBC); **Singapore Mutiny** (20.20 TV/Channel 4); **Pardes Abroad** (HR ENT); **The Bill** (Thames); **Khula Aangan** (Healthwise/BBC); and **Fall** (Meridian).

Film credits include: **The Mystic Masseur** (Merchant Ivory Productions); **My Son The Fanatic** (Zephyr Films/BBC); **Brothers in Trouble** (Renegade Films/BBC); **If It Don't Kill Ya...** (Magic Lamp Productions); **The Results** (SRK); and **Monk** (Imagine).

Radio credits include: **Like Another Mahabarata** (BBC Radio); and **Routes: A Journey of a Lifetime** (Radio Bremen).

Guy Rhys Nils

Guy graduated from the Drama Centre London.

Theatre credits include: **The Ramayana** (Birmingham Repertory Theatre and Royal National Theatre); **Transmissions** (Birmingham Repertory Theatre) and **Phoenix** (Royal Court).

Television and film credits include: **The Bill, Dalziel and Pascoe, The Apology, Big Bad World** and **A+E.**

Harvey Virdi Indira

Theatre credits include: **14 Songs, 2 Weddings & A Funeral** (Tamasha Theatre Company); **Letter From a Condemned Woman** (Royal Court); **When We Are Married, Romeo & Juliet, Square Circle** and **Playboy of the Asian World** (Leicester Haymarket); **Airport 2000** (Riverside Studios); **Twelfth Night** (British Council Tour, Zimbabwe); **Staying On** (Theatre of Comedy Tour); **A Yearning** (Birmingham Repertory Theatre and Lyric Hammersmith); **The Peacemaker** (Royal Theatre - Northampton); and **Romeo and Juliet** (Soapbox Theatre Company).

Television and film credits include: **House Across the Street** and **Casualty** (BBC); **Anita and Me** (Anita Productions); **Gran** (West End Central Films); **Guru in Seven** (Balhar Films); **Staying Alive** (LWT); **The Bill** (Thames); and **Bend It Like Beckham**.

Radio credits include: **Singh Tangos, Dancing Girls of Lahore, A Yearning** and **Samsara** (BBC); and **Shakti** (Watershed Productions).

Josephine Welcome Madhu

Theatre credits include: **The Disputation** (New End Theatre Hampstead); **Independence Day** and **Oh Sweet Sita** (Oval House Theatre); **Weisman and Copperface – A Jewish Western** (Traverse Theatre, Edinburgh); **Aureng-Zebe** and **A River Sutra** (Royal National Theatre Studio); **Wicked, Yaar!** and **Blood Wedding** (Royal National Theatre); **Sakuntala** and **Struggle of the Black Man and The Dogs** (Gate

Theatre); **Top Girls** and **Gasping** (Theatre Royal, Northampton); **The Servant of Two Masters** (Warehouse Theatre, Croydon); **Quartet** (Royal Lyceum Theatre); **Mein Kampf – Farce** (Newcastle Playhouse); **Comedy Without Title** and **Obscene Fables** (The Young Vic); and **The House of The Spirits** (West Yorkshire Playhouse).

Television credits include: **EastEnders, The Secret Slave, Dangerfield, Amongst Barbarians, Only Fools and Horses** and **Tenko** (BBC); **Pork Pie** (Channel 4); **Inspector Morse** (ITV); **Children's Ward** and **Jewel in the Crown** (Granada); and **The Bill** (Carlton).

Radio credits include: **Amongst Barbarians, Ananda Sananda** and **Bhowani Junction** (BBC).

Creatives

Ian Brown Director

Ian Brown is Associate Artistic Director at the West Yorkshire Playhouse, where he has directed **Eden End, Stepping Out, Broken Glass, The Comedy of Errors, Proposals, You'll Have Had Your Hole** and **Of Mice and Men**.

Theatre credits include: **Equus** (Beer Sheva Theatre, Israel); **Goodnight Children Everywhere**, which won the Olivier Award for Best New Play, and **Victoria** (RSC); **Five Kinds of Silence** (Out of the Blue Productions); **Strangers on a Train** (Colchester, Guildford and Richmond); **Babycakes** (Drill Hall); **Fool for Love** (Donmar Warehouse); **Widows** (Traverse Theatre); **Steaming** (Piccadilly Theatre); **Nabokov's Gloves** (Hampstead Theatre); **Killing Rasputin** (Bridewell Theatre); the original production of **Trainspotting** (Citizen's Theatre and The Bush Theatre).

From 1988 to 1999 Ian was Artistic Director and Executive Director of the Traverse Theatre, Edinburgh. Productions included: **Reader**, **The Collection**, **Unidentified Human Remains and the True Nature of Love** and **Poor Super Man** (Evening Standard Award); **Ines de Castro** and **Light in the Village**; **Moscow Stations** with Tom Courtenay (Evening Standard Award, Best Actor); **Hanging the President** (Scotsman Fringe First); **The Bench** and **Hardie and Baird**; **Bondagers** by Sue Glover (which transferred to the Donmar Warehouse and World Stage Festival, Toronto); and **Shining Souls**.

Ian was also Artistic Director of TAG Theatre Company, Citizens' Theatre for five years, where productions included: **Othello, A Midsummer Night's Dream, As You Like It, Romeo and Juliet, Hard Times, Can't Pay? Won't Pay!** and **Great Expectations**.

Television credits include 6 episodes of **EastEnders** (BBC).

Belinda Ackermann Designer

Belinda Ackermann has been resident designer at the Leicester Haymarket and Bristol Old Vic, as well as head of design at Derby Playhouse. She designed 54 shows at these 3 venues. Since 1987, as a freelance designer, she has worked at Theatre Royal Plymouth, Greenwich Theatre, Gate Theatre London, Riverside Studios London, Worcester Swan, Oldham Coliseum, Liverpool Playhouse, Leicester Haymarket, Library and Forum Theatres Manchester, Nuffield Theatre Southampton, RADA, Guildhall School of Music & Drama among others. She has also designed extensively for dance and film, and has taught on a part time basis at Goldsmith University & Central St. Martin's School of Art where she trained.

Faroque Khan Movement Director

Faroque also works as an actor and teacher.

Theatre credits include: **Unsuitable Girls** (Pilot Theatre); **Faustus Lite** (Rose Theatre Company); **Pandora's Box** (Pan Theatre UK – National Tour); **Rumble Fish** and **Lord of the Flies** (Pilot Theatre Company); **Twelfth Night** (Royal National Theatre Education Department); **Caucasian Chalk Circle** (Royal National Theatre/Theatre De Complicite); **Josie's Boys** (Red Ladder National Tour); **A Yearning** (Birmingham Repertory Theatre and Tamasha Theatre Company); **Safar So Far** (Fablevision Theatre Company, Glasgow); **The Gatekeepers Wife** (Alarmist Theatre Company); **Romeo and Juliet** (West Theatre, Glasgow); and **The Sound of Silence** (New Stage Theatre Company, Glasgow).

Television and Film credits include: **Umnachtung** (Distant Dreams); **Kismet Road** (Rod Natkiel Associates); **Inspector Rebus** (Scottish TV); **Ruth Rendell** (Blue Heaven); **Sound of Silence** (STV); and **Walking with Cavemen** (BBC).

Radio credits include: **Samsara** and **A Yearning** (BBC).

Ash Kotak Writer

Ash was born in North London and trained at the London International Film School. He has written, produced and/ or directed both drama and documentary including: **Macheath** and **Divided by Rape** (Channel 4); and **When Shura Cherkassky met Hobie** (BBC Radio 3). He has won a number of awards. His other projects have included **Maa** (a collaboration with Moti Roti, performed at the Royal Court in 1995), and **No Pain, No Gain** (written for the RSC's **New Shorts Now** project and performed at The Other Place in 1998). **Hijra** was his first full-length play. He has recently been commissioned to write plays for the Royal National Theatre Studio and the Theatre Royal Plymouth.

Mic Pool Sound Designer

In a twenty-four-year career in theatre sound Mic has been resident at the Lyric Theatre Hammersmith, the Royal Court, Tyne Theatre Company, and toured internationally with Ballet Rambert. He has designed the sound for over 200 productions including more than 100 for the West Yorkshire Playhouse where he is currently Director of Creative Technology. He received a TMA Award in 1992 for Best Designer (Sound) for **Life Is a Dream** and was nominated for both the Lucille Lortel and the Drama Desk Award for Outstanding Sound Design 2001 for the New York production of **The Unexpected Man**.

Recent theatre includes: **Art** (West End, Broadway and worldwide); **Shockheaded Peter** (Cultural Industry World Tour and West End); **The**

Unexpected Man (West End and Broadway); **Another Country** (Arts Theatre); **Dead Funny** (Nottingham Playhouse); **Hijra** (Theatre Royal Plymouth and The Bush); **A Midsummer Night's Dream, The Seagull, Victoria, Romeo and Juliet** and **Twelfth Night** (Royal Shakespeare Company); **The Seagull, The Tempest, Smoking With Lulu, Naked Justice, Broken Glass, Inconceivable, Johnson Over Jordan, Dangerous Corner, Eden End** and **Horse & Carriage** (West Yorkshire Playhouse).

Video work for theatre includes: **Johnson Over Jordan** (West Yorkshire Playhouse); **Dangerous Corner** (West Yorkshire Playhouse and Garrick Theatre, London); **Singin' In The Rain** (West Yorkshire Playhouse and Royal National Theatre); **The Turk in Italy** and **Il Trovatore** (ENO); and **Das Rheingold** (New National Theatre Tokyo).

Television includes the sound design for **How Wide Is Your Sky?** (Channel Four).

Tim Skelly Lighting Designer

Tim Skelly is a resident theatre designer and academic at the Workshop Theatre, University of Leeds. He has also worked as an academic at University College Bretton Hall in Wakefield and as a resident practitioner and teacher of lighting design at the Royal Academy of Dramatic Art in London.

As a freelance Lighting Designer recent professional credits include: **Union Street, The Lost Domain** and **Brother Jacques** (Theatre Royal Plymouth); **The Coming of Age** (Janet Smith and Dancers tour); **Korczak** (Teatr Muzyczny, Gdynia and Warsaw, Poland); **Ho! Ho! Ho!** (West Yorkshire Playhouse); **Having a Ball** (York Theatre Royal and Colchester Mercury); **Shades, Clean** and **Static** (Fringe First winner 2000 and British Council Tour to Harare, Zimbabwe); and **Neutrino** (Fringe First Winner 2001 for Unlimited Theatre); **Chiaroscuro, Plunge, Somewhere Inside** and **High Land** (Scottish Dance Theatre); **She is as She Eats** and **Time Taking Blush** (The Peter Darrell Foundation).

Tim also works as a lighting consultant for Yorkshire Sculpture Park and has collaborated with several artists, working on lighting designs for Sir Anthony Caro's *The Trojan Wars*, and retrospectives for Philip King and Christo.

Chris Yandell Assistant Director

Chris is currently studying Dramaturgy at Bretton Hall in Wakefield. Previous credits as Assistant Director include **Broken Glass** (West Yorkshire Playhouse), also for Ian Brown. He was previously Artistic Director of *Cult 45* Theatre Company.

Introduction

Ash Kotak

Hijra became a comedy because this was the perfect genre in which to highlight the taboo subject of homosexuality within the Asian community, both in the Sub-Continent and in the new countries we have made our homes and to which we have imported our culture as well as its prejudices.

Hijra was born as a result of going to the theatre since childhood. I grew up watching plays performed in Gujarati in Mumbai theatres, as well as in UK theatres performed here by newly emigrated Gujarati actors. My parents were part of this emerging theatre as were many of their friends. I loved sitting through read-throughs, rehearsals and performances. Sometimes I would be given the job of selling programmes – after all it was a family affair.

I saw wonderful plays, full of joy, laughter, tears and larger than life characters - *Pygmalion, Run for your Wife, The Rivals* (all adapted to suit Indian taste) and numerous hilarious and tragic plays by Indian writers.

I was born and brought up in the leafy suburbs of North London and here on stage was an India which I could understand and love; as a child I found 'going home' far too much to handle – the noise, the crowds, the heat, the cockroaches and mosquitoes, the endless monuments and photographs and so many relatives! To top it all my sisters and I would miss Christmas.

But in the theatre how the audiences would laugh. Comedy would be utilized to highlight social issues and injustice and performed to a quite conservative Gujarati community – in Mumbai it is normal for the audience, at the end of a performance, to leave a theatre without bothering to applaud the often very excellent actors. It may appear somewhat ungenerous but their logic is 'we paid to be entertained, we were and now it is time to go home'.

Hijra will not be performed in Mumbai unless I do some serious editing. It has been read by the Artistic Directors of a number of leading producing theatres. They liked it but added that today their hands are tied; the present Hindu fundamentalist Government would not allow such a play to be performed as it stands. The obviously gay bits would have to be cut out and there is no point having half a play performed.

Hijra was never meant to be controversial and was written with a conservative audience in mind. I, of course, want the play to be accessible to as many people as possible of any gender, race, culture and sexuality. Having said that, it is not politically correct and I'm pleased to see that so far the play has managed to appeal to all kinds of people.

Hijra concerns itself with identity. It is only when we are true to ourselves that we can hope to find real happiness. Yep that old chestnut! It is also a play about hypocrisy. How can Hindus accept the Hijra (eunuchs) but not gay people? But above all *Hijra* is a romantic comedy with the obligatory feelgood ending.

Hijra

Soon after its conception, I attended a reading of *Hijra* at the Riverside Studios in London, and found myself, quite spontaneously, fluctuating between lumps in my throat and a belly full of laughter! The social and political balance between the various genders in India is handled with great sensitivity and a wonderful sense of humour.

In a Hindu fundamentalist, male-dominated society all 'minorities' – whether they be women or female children, Muslim or Christian, gay, bisexual or transexual – face forms of oppression and brutality under a legal system that has not changed since the days of Oscar Wilde in Victorian England. The system of retribution and punishment remains intact, encouraging bribery, corruption, violence and blackmail – *it is still illegal to be gay in India.*

Hijra is a refreshing insight into such a social order. It is thought-provoking and portrays levels of love in a way that the middle class in India – shaped by Victorian values – find hard to take. Previous to the advent of this puritanical intrusion into our culture both Hijras and Devdasis (temple prostitutes) were honoured and revered.

The 'modernisation' of the Indian economy, under the leadership of a fundamentalist feudal government, has led to wide-scale riots and much bloodshed throughout the country. This systematic attack (on individuals and on communities) has taken a huge toll in terms of human suffering. Many a life has been taken or ruined because of these prejudices. The laws governing the gay community in India need closer scrutiny because they are a fundamental breach of human rights, by any standards in the twenty-first century.

Mala Sen
September 2000

Mala wrote the award-winning book Bandit Queen *which was translated across the globe, selling millions. The film of the book, released in the early 1990s, was also massively influential, winning awards worldwide. Her most recent book,* Death by Fire, *was published last year.*

ARTS FOR ALL AT THE WEST YORKSHIRE PLAYHOUSE

Since opening in 1990, the West Yorkshire Playhouse has established a reputation both nationally and internationally as one of Britain's most exciting and active producing theatres - winning awards for everything from its productions to its customer service. The Playhouse provides both a thriving focal point for the communities of West Yorkshire and theatre of the highest standard for audiences throughout the region and beyond. It produces up to 16 of its own shows each year in its two auditoria and stages over 1000 performances, workshops, readings and community events, watched by over 250,000 people. The Playhouse regularly tours its productions around Britain and abroad.

Alongside its work on stage the Playhouse has an expansive and groundbreaking programme of education and community initiatives. As well as a busy foyer and restaurant which are home to a range of activities through the week, the Playhouse offers extensive and innovative education programmes for children and adults, a wide range of unique community projects and is engaged in the development of culturally diverse art and artists. It is this 'Arts for All' environment, as well as a high profile portfolio of international theatre, new writing for the stage and major productions with leading artists that has kept the Playhouse constantly in the headlines and at the forefront of the arts scene. Artistic Director Jude Kelly is a leading and visionary spokesperson for the arts, proving through the work of the Playhouse how theatre can play a critical role in society and the creative economy.

Charles Smith Head Chef
Michael Montgomery Sous Chef
Simon Armitage and **Linda Monaghan** Commis Chefs
Lee Moran Kitchen Porter
Louise Poulter Chef de Partie
Caron Hawley and **Esther Lewis** Kitchen Assistants
Andrew Cherry*, Gail Lambert, Carrie Edwards and **Kath Langton** Restaurant Assistants
Tara Dean-Tipple, Emma Ibbetson, Sarah Cremin, Victoria Dobson and **Victoria Burt** Catering Assistants*
Qamar Zaman, Jennifer Douglas and **Natalie Bailey** Coffee Shop Supervisors *
Malcolm Salsbury Bar Manager
Sally Thomas and **Hannah Thomas** Assistant Bar Managers
Helen Cawley, Emma Coulson, Alexander Malyou, Patricia McMahon, Nicola Milton, Emma Paling, David Sinclair, Graeme Thompson and **Jennie Webster** Bar Assistants*

Company and Stage Management

Diane Asken Company Manager
Paul Veysey and **Karen Whitting** Stage Managers
Porl Cooper, Hugh McInally and **Sarah Northcott** Deputy Stage Managers
Sarah Braybook, Nina Dilley, Christine Guthrie and **Toby Heaps** Assistant Stage Managers

Corporate Affairs

Daniel Bates Director of Corporate Affairs
Kate Jeeves Development Manager
Rachel Coles Head of Press
Catherine Twite Press Officer
Sarah Jennings Corporate Affairs Assistant

Finance

Caroline Harrison Finance Director
Teresa Garner Finance Manager
Coleen Anderson Finance Officer
Jenny Copley Cashier and Ledger Clerk
Susan Werbinski Salaries/Accounts Clerk

Literature

Alex Chisholm Literary and Events Manager

Marketing and Sales

Kate Sanderson Marketing Director
Nick Boaden Marketing Manager
John Polley Graphic Design and New Media Manager
Shirley Harvey Graphic Design Officer
Kevin Jamieson Marketing Officer – Networks
Stephen Downie Marketing Officer – Programmes
Emma Lowery Marketing Assistant*
Angela Robertson Sales Manager
Caroline Gornall Deputy Sales Manager
Lynn Hudson, Sarah Jennings, Emma Lowery, Ben Williams and **Mel Worman** Duty Supervisors
Carol Kempster Senior Box Office Assistant
Bronia Daniels, Maureen Kirkby, Libby Noble, Sally Thomas, Joy Johnson, Pene Hayward and **Philip Strafford** Box Office Assistants

THEATRE MANAGEMENT

Helen Child Theatre Manager
Karen Johnson House Manager
Lee Harris and **Sheila Howarth** Duty Managers
Joy Johnson Assistant Duty Manager
Asha France and **Bik Yuk Wan** Theatre Administrators

Housekeeping

Doreen Hartley Domestic Services Manager*
Mary Ambrose, Eddy Dube, Harold Hartley, Michaela Singleton, Paul Robinson, Teresa Singleton, Hong Yan Wang, Sarah Wonnacott and **Dabo Guan** Cleaners*

Security

Denis Bray and **Allan Mawson**

Customer Services

Kathy Dean, Jackie Gascoigne and **Leigh Exley**

Maintenance

Frank Monaghan Maintenance Manager
Jim Gaffigan, Martin McHugh and **Tony Wardle** Maintenance Assistants
Shane Montgomery General Services Assistant

Performance Staff

Andy Charlesworth and **Jon Murray** Firemen
Rebecca Ashdown, Jo-Anne Brown, Ruth Carnagie, Maia Daguerre, Jon Dean, Jennifer Douglas, Shaun Exley, Simon Howarth, Clare Kerrigan, Sally McKay, Hayley Mort, Jo Murray, Soazig Nicholson, Caroline Quinn, Alex Ramseyer, Genevieve Say, Luke Sherman, Jamie Steer, Tom Stoker, Devi Thaker, Mala Thaker, Tal Varma, Daneill Whyles, Jemal Cohen, Tanja Barge, Deborah Barker, Rachel Blakeby, James Whelan, Fynnwin Prager, Sangeeta Chana, Vinod France, Clare Kerrigan, Indy Panesar, Gummas Phull, Ian Woods, Kirsty Latham, Marcus Stewart and **Qamar Zaman** Attendants*
Beth Allan, Jackie Gascoigne, Clare Kerrigan and **Jessica Kingsley** Playhouse Hosts*

PRODUCTION

Production Management

Suzi Cubbage Production Manager
Eddie De Pledge Freelance Production Manager
Christine Alcock, Production Administrator

Carpenters' Shop

Dickon Harold Master Carpenter
Philip Watson Deputy Master Carpenter
Jimmy Ragg Carpenter
John Ashton and **Kevin Cassidy** Freelance Carpenter
Andrew Dye Metal Shop Supervisor

Paint Shop

Virginia Whiteley Head Scenic Artist
Donna Maria Taylor Scenic Artist

Production Electricians

Stephen Sinclair Chief Electrician
Julie Rebbeck Deputy Chief Electrician
Christopher Sutherland, Drew Wallis and **Melani Nicola** Electricians

Props Department

Chris Cully Head of Props
Scott Thompson, Susie Cockram and **Sarah Partridge** Prop Makers

Sound Department

Glen Massam Chief Sound Technician
Adrian Parker Deputy Sound Technician
Martin Pickersgill Sound Technician

Technical Stage Management

Martin Ross Technical Stage Manager
Michael Cassidy Senior Stage Technician
Julian Brown Stage Technician

Wardrobe Department

Stephen Snell Head of Wardrobe
Victoria Marzetti Deputy Head of Wardrobe
Julie Ashworth Head Cutter
Selina Nightingale Cutter
Alison Barrett Costume Prop Maker/ Dyer
Sarah Marsh and **Nicole Martin** Wardrobe Assistants
Anne-Marie Snowden Costume Hire Manager
Kim Freeland Wig Supervisor*
Vivian Brown Wardrobe Maintenance/ Head Dresser
Lisa Parkinson Wig Dresser

*Denotes part-time

CHARITABLE TRUSTS

Audrey and Stanley Burton 1960 Trust
The D'Oyly Carte Charitable Trust
The Emmandjay Charitable Trust
Harewood Charitable Settlement
Kenneth Hargreaves Charitable Trust
The Frances Muers Trust
L & D Cohen Trust
Clothworkers' Foundation

PROJECT SUPPORTERS

New Opportunities Fund SPARK and Cybercafe
The Heritage Lottery Fund Celebrating Memories
Lloyds TSB Foundation Skills Generation
Ragdoll Foundation Imaginary Worlds
BBC Northern Exposure

PRODUCTION THANKS

Mr Aslam of The Aagrah Restaurant and Hotel Group
Jill John at Air India
The Times Of India
Leeds Bradford International Airport

West Yorkshire Playhouse
Corporate Supporters

Sponsors of the Arts Development Unit

 PROVIDENT FINANCIAL

DIRECTORS' CLUB

Executive Level Members

      CARLSBERG-TETLEY   EVANS property group

Associate Level Members

Hammond Suddards Edge   **YORKSHIRE POST**

Director Level Members

Bacon & Woodrow	Lloyds TSB
Bank of Scotland	New Horizons
British Gas	Provident Financial
BWD Rensburg	True Temper
Crowne Plaza	Thompson Design
GNER	Yorkshire Bank
KPMG	Yorkshire Dales Ice Cream
Le Meridien Queens	Yorkshire Television

One Performance Sponsors

Singin' in the Rain

Singin' in the Rain

Inscape Investments
The Comedy of Errors

Horse & Carriage

If you would like to learn how your organisation can become involved with the success of the West Yorkshire Playhouse please contact the Corporate Affairs Department on 0113 213 7274/5 or email corporateaffairs@wyp.org.uk

First published in 2000 by Oberon Books Ltd
521 Caledonian Road, London N7 9RH
Tel: +44 (0) 20 7607 3637 / Fax: +44 (0) 20 7607 3629
e-mail: info@oberonbooks.com
www.oberonbooks.com

A catalogue record for this book is available from the British
Library.

PB ISBN: 9781840021912
E ISBN: 9781783192908

Cover design by Pierre et Gilles

Dedicated to David Prescott, dramaturge,
for his invaluable guidance

Special thanks to Hannah Kodicek,
Julia Parr and Ian Brown

Characters

SHEILA

INDIRA

MADHU

AUNTY

NILS

GURU HIJRA

HIJRA

RAJ
later as RANI

ANNOUNCER

BOBBY

MRS PATEL

Originally developed by the London New Play Festival, *Hijra* was first performed as a co-production at The Theatre Royal Plymouth on 19 October 2000, and then at The Bush Theatre on 15 November 2000, with the following cast:

SHEILA, Natalie Tinn

INDIRA, Sharon Maharaj

MADHU, Leena Dhingra

AUNTY/ANNOUNCER/MRS PATEL, Charubala Chokshi

NILS, Emil Marwa

GURU, Bhasker Patel

HIJRA/BOBBY, Rez Kempton

RAJ/RANI, Raj Ghatak

Director, Ian Brown

Designer, Bob Bailey

Lighting Designer, Aideen Malone

Sound, Mic Pool

Choreography, Jiva

ACT ONE

Scene 1

Bombay. Twilight.

As evening approaches and the Bombay heat reduces, the frantic sounds of traffic can be heard from a distance. Horns blow continuously and the song 'Chalte, Chalte' from the film 'Pakeezah' becomes prominent as we see a lone woman dancing. Or is it a woman? She is dressed in a brightly coloured silk sari, her jewellery glistens in the bright orange light of the setting sun. We see people but they are frozen and in shadow. RAJ watches from a distance.

Suddenly the people come alive and we see we are at a wedding. A shinai plays wedding music. NILS is with MADHU and AUNTY. SHEILA and her mother INDIRA are on a manhunt.

INDIRA: Top wedding. Absolutely everyone is here.

SHEILA points to someone at a distance.

SHEILA: He's cute. Who's that?

INDIRA: Sheila, he's no good. A rogue. I blame his parents, no control. He's ruined his family name. Oh look, there she is! Madhu Mehta. And that must be her son, Nils. I haven't seen him since he was this high.

She points at NILS.

SHEILA: Which one mum?

INDIRA: Over there! Open your eyes. Remember you met him in Nairobi when we were there. Nils. Such a sweet boy. He's living in Wembley now, just near us. Nils Mehta. They're looking for a girl for him.

SHEILA: Hm, cute.

INDIRA: His father is very rich, big businessman. And Nils has excellent prospects. He's a MBA from London

21

University. Just got a new job in the city. Very good boy. Come on. Hurry up, jaldi.

They wave at MADHU, NILS and AUNTY. The HIJRA dances.

INDIRA: Madhu. Arre! Is it you?

MADHU: Oh, look who it is. Indira. Can't be. Such a lovely surprise. You here in Bombay.

AUNTY: Mumbai.

INDIRA: (*To AUNTY.*) *Jaishri* Krishna.

AUNTY nods and gives a weak smile.

At weddings you never know whom you're going to bump into.

MADHU: Is this your Sheila? Look at her. So grown up. How are you beti?

SHEILA: Fine thank you masi. (*To NILS.*) Hi.

NILS: Hello.

MADHU: This is my Nils. This is Indira masi. And her lovely daughter Sheila. Such a lovely girl. (*To SHEILA.*) And this is aunty.

NILS: Hi.

MADHU: Last time we were together was in New York. Now whose wedding was it?

INDIRA: Yes. Well we all knew that would never last.

There is silence for a moment as they watch the HIJRA dance.

MADHU: The bride's my real niece.

INDIRA: Oh. Very lovely girl.

MADHU: Yes, poor thing. She's married into a good family.

INDIRA: Oh, the best. So rich but so down to earth people. Madhu, I tell you it's hard bringing up a daughter all alone.

AUNTY: You should get her married off.

MADHU: Yes. (*To SHEILA.*) Have you finished studying yet?

SHEILA: Yes.

INDIRA: She's a graduate.

MADHU: You'll be getting engaged soon. A pretty girl like you must have someone. Anyone special?

INDIRA: I'm looking for a boy for her. I want her to settle in London.

MADHU: We're looking too. (*To NILS.*) *Aren't we darling?*

INDIRA: Yes I know. We heard.

NILS: Mum! That's all you ever think about.

INDIRA: Don't you want to settle?

NILS: I'm happy being young, free and single. But who knows someone may sweep me off my feet.

MADHU and INDIRA laugh. SHEILA blushes.

INDIRA: Nils, we mothers worry. If we don't who else will? Hai ne Madhu?

MADHU: Yes. It's such a worry.

INDIRA: I'm so pleased Sheila and Nils have met again after all these years.

MADHU: (*To SHEILA.*) I used to change your nappies. (*To INDIRA.*) Where are you staying in Bombay?

AUNTY: Arreh! Mumbai. Mumbai.

INDIRA: At the Taj of course.

MADHU: Just near us. Very good. You must come home while you're here.

INDIRA: Call us.

MADHU: Yes, yes. Definitely.

INDIRA: Must mingle. Lovely seeing you.

SHEILA: Bye aunty. (*To AUNTY.*) Aunty.

MADHU: Goodbye beti.

AUNTY: Jaishri Krishna.

SHEILA: Bye Nils.

NILS: Bye Sheila. Nice to meet you.

MADHU: See you soon. See you soon. What a lovely girl.

SHEILA and INDIRA walk off as MADHU, NILS and
AUNTY watch the HIJRA.

INDIRA: (*Whispering.*) It's good for us to play hard to get.
Well done. She's keen.

SHEILA: Nils is nice.

INDIRA: Top boy. He's a perfect match.

SHEILA: Mum, we don't know that yet.

INDIRA: Ha! Forget about all those romantic notions of
falling in love. Leave that to the movies. We're talking
about marriage here. Understand one thing, there is no
such thing as the right man. You have to go for the best.

SHEILA: Maybe he doesn't want me.

INDIRA: Think positive! You're a negative thinking
person. Of course he wants you. Bust and bum is all men
want and you have ample of both, thank God.

SHEILA: Thanks!

INDIRA: If you fail now, what will you do? This is your
last chance. Most of the good boys are long married or
hooked up. We are lucky that Nils is still available, it's a
miracle. He is not going to slip out of our hands. We're
on a good wicket here. Now come on in case we find
something better. Jaldi. Look who it is, absolutely
everyone is here. Hello.

RAJ: (*To the HIJRA.*) You're not drawing enough attention to yourself.

HIJRA: What can I do? They're in their own world.

RAJ: Flaunt yourself more. Be more suggestive. Lewd, crude and rude. We need the money.

HIJRA: The stingy good-for-nothings.

RAJ: Flirt with the boys. Their egos drive them to revel in the attention whilst their machismo forces them to repel it. They'll pay easily and quickly. (*Pointing towards NILS.*) See that hot guy over there? Dance for him.

The HIJRA dances crudely and flirts with NILS who tries to ignore her. MADHU takes some money out of her purse.

AUNTY: What are you doing?

MADHU: We had better give the hijra at least one hundred rupees.

AUNTY: Arreh! So much. Five rupees will do.

MADHU: We don't want to bring bad luck to Nils. We must give at least seventy.

AUNTY: Okay. Okay. But fifty rupees is enough.

NILS: Thanks.

They look around.

AUNTY: Hm! These Mumbai girls, look at them there! Shocking. *Khy sharem nathi.* Shameless. Isn't that, you know, what is her name? From Chicago. Money and education is no substitute for a good family background. Her background bankrupt completely. Totally Westernized. I blame her parents, they were too liberal. Don't know ABC about anything and end up becoming ABCDs.

AUNTY and MADHU laugh.

NILS: American born confused desis. Yawn.

MADHU: Ha. ABCDs. EFG.

NILS: Eh?

MADHU: American born confused desis emigrated from Gujarat.

AUNTY and MADHU laugh.

AUNTY: You know I heard they put things in the coc, the American coc.

MADHU is confused and embarrassed.

NILS: Coke.

AUNTY: Yes coc. What is wrong with our own Indian coc? It is cheaper and much better and made in India.

The HIJRA passes near them and she flirts raunchily with NILS. MADHU and AUNTY laugh. AUNTY gives her money.

NILS: Why is Aunty giving the hijra money?

MADHU: They have the power to grant wishes and cast spells.

Scene 2

The hijra home, Grant Road, Mumbai. Day.

The HIJRA remains dancing watched by the GURU HIJRA. We are in a large, almost empty room in need of redecoration.

GURU: Ta the thi tum and turn. I have told you a thousand times. Grace, charm and style with mystique, not this modern way lewd…

HIJRA: Crude and rude.

GURU: Okay clever clogs. Now dance.

The HIJRA dances, does it right for a while and then does it wrong again.

Oh, oh oh. Start again. Again.

RAJ enters.

Hello darling.

The HIJRA flirts with him and giggles.

RAJ: Hello Mina Kumari.

GURU: Raj, don't encourage her. Dance, dance. You are meant to evoke a feeling of awe and at the same time fear, you stupid girl.

HIJRA: I'm tired.

GURU: I will take a cane to you. Raj is a better dancer than you and he's not even one of us. You will continue doing it until you get it right, now ta the thi tum.

RAJ: Maa, she's trying. It's not her fault that our cashbox is almost empty. We haven't been doing very well lately.

GURU: Ha, I'm not surprised. Thank god the wedding season has started. (*To the young HIJRA.*) Class and sex appeal!

The HIJRA dances crudely.

RAJ: Maa, the priests at all the Mandirs refuse to give us details of the new births nor a list of the weddings at which they are officiating. They want more money this year. And if we don't pay them, we won't know who's getting married and who's been born. And so we can't make any money.

GURU: What about Bababapa?

RAJ: No. I've tried.

GURU: We have made him thousands and thousands of rupees over the years.

RAJ: He said we're no longer a viable business proposition. He says that other hijra houses make him more money.

GURU: Do you have to use that derogatory word?

RAJ: It's a word. The more we use it, the less meaning it holds. That is what you are, after all.

The HIJRA dances crudely wriggling her bottom.

GURU: Stop! Stop! Get out of my sight. This is a respectable household, if you want to act like a common whore go live on the streets. The shame you bring on this house.

HIJRA: Sorry Guruji. It's just I'm so bushed.

GURU: Get out, go and cook dinner. Is this the thanks I get? I treat her as if she were my own daughter.

The HIJRA exits.

RAJ: You do push her too hard.

GURU: How else will she ever learn? She shuns tradition… this very house is the champion of our heritage, her heritage, a place where our customs have been refined and preserved. In my day we revered the honour of being from such a house. We were totally dedicated to our Guru, may she rest in peace. One would never dare even to look at her eye to eye. Now look at us today, Ha. We were famous and devotees…

RAJ: Hijras.

GURU: And there were many, from this house, this very house were invited to be confidants in palaces all over India…the respect… Our value was such they would shower us with gold and precious jewels. Only we alone had the same right as the Maharaja or Nawab. Access to the whole palace. Free to walk amongst the men and the women, as advisers, guards, entertainers and sometimes lovers. Don't you forget it? We were diplomats and counsellors, privy to all secrets. The smooth running of the kingdoms depended on our propriety. So we were rewarded…but then the damn British left.

RAJ: Yes, Maa but times have changed. Today the people expect a little sexual innuendo, in fact they enjoy it. Even the priests tell me that we have to change our ways. Lewd, crude and rude. Survival of the fittest.

GURU: Never! Never, as long as I live! Your job is to manage this house and that's all.

RAJ: But how can I when we don't have enough money coming in. I try my best but without finances. Even the mafia gundas are being very demanding nowadays. They want more money too. We have to adapt to the times.

GURU: Leave the artistry to me okay. We manage. Do you go without anything? I am an ambassador. Would you ask Shikandi herself to lay down her weapons on the great battlefield? The Pandavas' victory is ours too, don't you ever forget that. Are you really asking me to run a whorehouse? I'd rather rot away in poverty!

RAJ: Well, that's settled. We will just have to give the priests more money. But that will break into your savings for your future, which I have invested to give you an income when you choose to retire.

GURU: Oh do you always have to talk about money.

RAJ: Maa don't stress yourself. You'll become ill. One day I'll take you away from here and then you can live like a queen.

GURU: To England? With you and your lover?

RAJ is surprised.

You love him, I know. I want you to settle down. I do worry about you. You were such a vulnerable boy when I found you and such lovely rosy cheeks.

She affectionately pinches his cheek.

RAJ: Oh, Maa.

GURU: My dreams were answered, my own son. You were sent to me by Goddess Bahuchara Maa herself. I was to save you, to rescue you from a life of prostitution and pimps. Those cruel people. We hijras gathered around and cursed those scoundrels using our greatest tools, shame and public humiliation. They were our weapons.

That is the time to be crude, rude and lewd! We raised our saris to flash our sacred and mutilated genitalia. In return you ended my loneliness, darling. Now it is time for you to fly the nest.

RAJ: Maa I won't leave you.

GURU: Nonsense. I'll be okay. I'm a survivor. Bahuchara Maa will help me. I'm not worried about the future. All I want is for you to be happy, darling.

RAJ: But how will you manage?

GURU: Now don't you fret about that? I want you to see the world. I want you to do all of those things I dreamed of. Rome, Paris, Venice, Southall, Wembley...

RAJ: They won't give me a visa to get into England.

GURU: Well that settles it. You won't be able to go then.

RAJ: Maa!

They both laugh.

GURU: If I hadn't been such a fool, I'd have saved the money to send you to Oxford or Cambridge. But there you are I've always been an extravagant old fool.

RAJ: Maa, you've done more than enough for me.

GURU: Ah, England. Marmite, Twinings Tea, Quaker Oats, HP Sauce. And Shakespeare, Kears, Hardy, Enid Blyton. I read somewhere that English people only go to the toilet once a week.

RAJ: Because they're so uptight?

GURU: It's those toilets they have there, ghastly.

RAJ: What?

GURU: How do they go to the toilet? I mean if they don't squat, how do they build up the pressure?

Scene 3

Mumbai taxi. Same day.

AUNTY is reading the 'Times of India' matrimonial column.

MADHU: You've got my looks and your father's brain.

AUNTY: The best boy. Arreh how many boys are there like our Nils? You can't find one anywhere. We can get the best for him. MBA, money, white skin, British Passport.

She looks at the newspaper.

NILS: Good asset, aren't I?

AUNTY: How are you driving idiot? These taxiwala's nowadays. *Grooms wanted for... Punjabi* oh no. American passport would be better of course, nowadays everyone wants American passport. *Muslim*, no, no. Here. *Hindu Gujarati...* Oh, this sounds good. *Alliance with horoscope and full size photo, invited from parents of well educated fair professional Brahmin boy of affluent family. No vices. For twenty-one year old girl.* It's good, she's young. We can train her still. *Five foot six, slim...*

MADHU: Yes.

AUNTY: *Fair/wheatish.*

NILS: Wheatish?

AUNTY: Colour. *Charming, beautiful, vegetarian, cultured, convent educated, professional, religious, docile...*

NILS: Docile!

MADHU: Yes homemaker, just the sort of girl I would like. She will help me with the housework and cooking. And give me a bit of company.

AUNTY: Eh, taxiwala, drive slower. Chup, shut up, don't talk. Arreh, these people you are polite to them and then they take liberties. It's good for a try... *Apply with full biodata.*

NILS: What's that?

AUNTY: Biodata means biodata.

MADHU: CV.

AUNTY: Oh, no, *USA preferred*. I told you.

NILS: Sorry.

AUNTY: We will have to try the Internet.

MADHU: I have my heart set on Sheila.

AUNTY: Ha, her mother Indira! You wouldn't believe that her husband has just died. Those bright new silk saris…those colours.

She tuts.

MADHU: He's been dead for over a year.

AUNTY: It might be okay in your third-class Africa but when you people come back to India you should learn to act like proper Indians.

MADHU: You don't know what you are talking about.

AUNTY: Ha! You just don't know how to talk full stop.

They are silent.

NILS: Now, now you two.

AUNTY: That girl Sheila has never worked in her life.

MADHU: She's a smart girl. She has a degree.

AUNTY: Maybe so. But do we want Nils to marry a non-performing asset? (*To NILS.*) Do you?

NILS: Forget it. I'm not interested. Do we have to go on about marriage all the time? God!

MADHU: Indira's a very smart woman. She took lots of money from her husband, when he was alive, and invested it. She's clever, not stupid like me. Insurance in case he left it to all his girlfriends or god knows whom.

AUNTY: How much money has she got?

MADHU: Over five hundred thousand pounds I heard.

AUNTY: Oh! But why isn't she married yet?

MADHU: She had a failed engagement, someone was telling me.

AUNTY: She's unfit. I told you.

NILS: Very good girl, very bad boy. Gossip, gossip, gossip…

AUNTY: It's not gossip. It's analysing the facts. If they didn't have secrets they'd be nothing to work out.

NILS: It's cruel and unfair.

MADHU: This is for your benefit.

NILS: Is that why you're forcing me into getting married?

AUNTY: We are not your enemies.

MADHU: We want you to be happy darling.

AUNTY: At least see some girls. What is wrong, nothing to lose?

MADHU: If you don't like them just say no. And we will find other girls.

AUNTY: Listen, beta. You have to get married some time.

MADHU: What is there without marriage and children?

AUNTY: Is there someone already?

NILS: No! No.

AUNTY: I blame you Madhu. You've been too liberal with the boy.

MADHU: In my day we got married for the sex.

AUNTY: Madhu! Enough! Taxiwala why are you taking so long? Jaldi. Jaldi. (*To MADHU.*) You are leaving tomorrow and nothing is settled.

NILS: Oh stop! Stop! Stop!

The driver does an emergency stop.

AUNTY: (*To the driver.*) Not you idiot!

The driver drives again.

MADHU: He's a good boy. He'll sort himself out.

AUNTY: What can I do!

NILS: Why can't you just let me do whatever I want to do?

AUNTY: Shut up, don't talk. Marry a nice girl…

MADHU: And then do whatever you like.

Scene 4

Juhu Beach. Night.

The moon is full and the stars shine brightly. Cars and voices can be heard in the distance behind the sound of the ocean. NILS and RAJ meet and hug.

NILS: Raj.

RAJ: Nils.

NILS: Raj.

RAJ: Nils.

NILS: Raj.

RAJ: Nils.

NILS: Yes.

RAJ: Has anyone ever told you how gorgeous you are?

NILS: Yes all the time. Christ, I'm so happy to see you.

They both laugh and hug again.

RAJ: Why didn't you talk to me at the wedding?

NILS: Well that's a bit obvious.

RAJ: At least an acknowledgement would have been nice. The hijra went all gooey for you. She thought you were hot.

NILS: Yeah thanks a lot for that.

They laugh.

RAJ: Why couldn't you see me in the last few days? It's your last week here.

NILS: Sorry.

Silence.

Juhu Beach is so dirty now and it used to be so lovely. I remember when I came here as a kid. It was like paradise after all the craziness of the rest of the city.

RAJ: Great.

NILS: Did you know that close to water the negative and positive ions in the atmosphere are absolutely equal thus creating a heightened feeling of balance.

RAJ: Stop changing the subject!

NILS: It's just been one event after another. This aunty and that uncle. Weddings and parties. The same old questions and then the biggi, when are you getting married.

RAJ: And how do you answer them?

NILS: I tell them I'm happily married to an unsuitable but beautiful boy who I met two months ago whilst cruising Chapatti Beach.

RAJ: Chowpati Beach. What do you mean me unsuitable?

He hugs NILS.

NILS: Stop it will you!

RAJ: You're so uptight.

Silence.

Why don't you just tell people the truth?

NILS: Raj.

RAJ: People who really love you will still love you.

NILS: I should just marry a girl and have the occasional shag with a guy. Then everyone will be happy.

RAJ: Really!

NILS is silent.

Give me a kiss. I dare you.

RAJ goes to kiss NILS who pulls away.

NILS: People are watching.

RAJ: So, who cares? You don't know any of them.

NILS: No.

RAJ: Okay. I'm only teasing you. I love you Nils.

NILS: Raj…it hasn't been like this with a bloke before.

RAJ: If we want it to work we're going to have to fight. Don't you want us to be together? Hm, a house in the country…another in London…parties…

NILS: Of course I want that but…it's so difficult… We have to be practical. We both knew the score from the beginning.

RAJ: But we couldn't predict what was going to happen. Sorry I don't have as much control over my emotions as you do. You English are so cold and reserved.

NILS: I'm not English! What can I do about it, eh? I'll come back each year and we can email and phone.

RAJ: Ha! Great! Hot male dot COM! It's impossible to maintain a long distance relationship. The solution is simple. You can come and live in India.

NILS: We've been over this. It's nothing to do with you but I could never be happy here. We have to find a way for you to come to London.

RAJ: If I was a woman and we married, I could've come to the UK as your wife. It's so unfair.

They are silent.

NILS: I'm just trying to make it easier for us when I have to leave. I want to stay with you but it's impossible.

RAJ: Maa wants to meet you tomorrow in the evening. There's a celebration.

NILS: Come on let's find a hotel.

RAJ: I want you to meet her. Please.

NILS: Yes. I promise. Tomorrow.

RAJ: Okay sourpuss.

NILS: Sourpuss?

RAJ: Come on.

Scene 5

NILS' aunt's home. Later the same day.

MADHU, AUNTY, INDIRA and SHEILA sit drinking tea.

INDIRA: She is a good girl and does what she is told. But don't think I would ever force her into something she didn't want to do. But I want to know, is your Nils seeing other girls?

MADHU: No. With such a lovely girl here why would he want to? I was just telling Nils only yesterday how lovely she is.

SHEILA: Thank you.

INDIRA: I want an answer. We can't hang around. These are important matters, but we thought we would give you first choice. She is a good catch and these are competitive times. You can't afford to miss an opportunity. Ten 'O' Levels, 3 'A' Levels, a Degree…in Child Care.

MADHU/AUNTY: Oh.

INDIRA: Indian finishing school. She speaks fluent Gujarati and Hindi. She can also write.

MADHU/AUNTY: Oh.

INDIRA: And she plays the piano and the sitar. Grade seven.

MADHU/AUNTY: Grade seven.

INDIRA: And most important she is still a virgin.

MADHU/AUNTY: Well done. Very good girl.

SHEILA: Thank you.

MADHU: My Nils and Sheila are made for each other but…

INDIRA: That is why we are here.

MADHU: I can't make a decision for my son…

INDIRA: I am being very accommodating. Your family has had its fair share of scandal.

MADHU: Well! Speak for yourself.

AUNTY: Madhu, it's a parent's duty to guide their children.

INDIRA: Now please don't take it the wrong way. I do admire women who can put up with their husband's infidelities. Men just don't appreciate how women can adapt when they have been thrown aside.

SHEILA: Mum!

MADHU: Indira, what…

AUNTY: We have to accept it and at least be grateful that they do all that stuff outside the home. It's when they break up the family. That is the wrong thing to do.

MADHU: At least it's more honest. (*To INDIRA.*) Unlike some people's husband.

INDIRA: Well!

AUNTY: It's our duty as women, yours and mine to preserve our families and uphold values. It's even more important for you people living abroad. Our work is hard and, as you both know, we cannot always rely on men.

MADHU: In Africa we kept our own culture thank you.

INDIRA: And we've been there for donkey's years.

AUNTY: But in Africa you're hardly going to mix with those blacks. It's when you go to the West the problems start. You know our Indian mentality. White is right, brown stay around, black stay back. That's how we Asians have become so successful abroad.

MADHU: But it's that success that goes to a man's head.

INDIRA: Yes. Their inferiority complex shifts into a superiority complex.

MADHU: Flip sides of the same coin.

INDIRA: When we married them they were penniless. We struggled to live and save but as soon as things were a little bit okay, he's off. He wants his lost bachelor years back, with the girls and drink and whatever.

MADHU: Get it out of their system before they are married. It makes it better for the woman later.

AUNTY: Madhu! Shut up! Don't talk!

INDIRA: (*Laughing.*) Are you saying your Nils is like that?

MADHU: No! My Nils is different. He isn't the type of boy to waste his time with lots of silly girls and he doesn't drink. It's not that he's not popular. But he never sits idle doing nothing, never. He's busy with his books, hobbies and work. He's always having friends stay over after they've worked late. So many boys. Popular that's my son.

INDIRA: He'll make an excellent husband. But if you have an objection for some reason, we will go elsewhere.

MADHU: No of course not. I will talk to him, I promise. I like your Sheila and Nils' father and I would be happy for an engagement to take place. And Nils is a good boy; he'll do as I tell him. And I've already talked to him about you beti.

SHEILA: Thank you.

They hug each other as NILS enters the room.

NILS: Hello, sorry I'm late. Oh! Hi.

MADHU: Oh you're going to live for a hundred years. We were just talking about you.

SHEILA: Hi.

NILS: Hi Sheila.

INDIRA: Aren't we having fun, all of us together in India?

NILS: Yeah, it's all right. Couldn't live here though, it'd drive me mad.

AUNTY: India is great.

INDIRA: Are you going back soon?

NILS: In a few days.

INDIRA: We'll be back in Wembley soon too. We were going to the US but there's no need now. Hai ne Madhu? And we'll have dinner Nils. You should taste her cooking. She was trained by a chef at the Taj hotel here in Bombay. She did a summer course.

MADHU/AUNTY: Oh.

AUNTY: Nils, why don't you go onto the balcony so you can talk to each other, alone.

INDIRA: Yes, so you youngsters can get to know each other.

NILS: No, no. We're okay here.

MADHU: Go, go. (*To SHEILA.*) Nils is shy. Go.

NILS and SHEILA go to the balcony.

There is a beautiful naivety about her.

AUNTY: Yes she is so docile.

INDIRA: And he's a good boy, very sober in his nature. We'll have lovely grandchildren.

Meanwhile on the balcony.

SHEILA: I love India. I've done heaps of shopping.

NILS: Great.

SHEILA: But I've only bought things I really loved and which were reasonable. You've got to be careful. They think us foreigners have loads of money.

NILS: Yeah, you've gotta be on the ball.

SHEILA: That's me though. Very cost conscious.

NILS: Good Indian girl.

SHEILA: That's me. Are you laughing at me?

NILS: No. It's good to be careful. So what are the three witches plotting in there? Sorry I didn't mean your mum was a witch.

SHEILA laughs.

SHEILA: What do you think?

NILS: Marriage, marriage, marriage. Oh! My God!

SHEILA: Why did you agree to see me?

NILS: I didn't. Did I?

SHEILA: There seems to have been a misunderstanding.

She gets up to leave.

NILS: Stay. Please. I didn't mean to embarrass you. I'm sorry. Are you looking forward to going back to Wembley?

SHEILA: Are you? It's just I'm having such a good time here. That's me though, I have fun and a good time wherever I go. I'm like that. Very easy… Oh God! I am so stupid.

NILS: No you're not. It's not good to put yourself down. You seem really bright to me.

SHEILA laughs nervously.

Don't you think you are?

SHEILA shrugs.

NILS: You're not used to compliments are you?

SHEILA laughs again.

SHEILA: It's just most men like me for other reasons.

NILS: Because you're very pretty.

SHEILA: Now enough of that.

NILS: I like bright people.

SHEILA: It puts some guys off.

NILS: That depends on whom you're trying to impress.

SHEILA: You're quite a modern man, aren't you. I like that.

NILS: I like to think of myself as quite sorted.

SHEILA: You're different to how I imagined you to be.

NILS: So what did you think I was going to be like?

SHEILA: Don't know. I suppose I thought you'd be arrogant and chauvinistic.

NILS: I could be for all you know.

SHEILA: No. I don't think you're like that. You're quite sweet.

NILS: Sweet. Yuck! Sounds a bit wet.

SHEILA: No I mean it in a good way. Honestly. How did you imagine me to be?

NILS: I don't know.

SHEILA: Are you involved with somebody already?

NILS: No. No!

SHEILA: So aren't you the marrying kind?

NILS: Yes. Yes I am. Of course but I'm not desperate. To get married that is. I'm not saying you are either. It's just I don't know what I'm saying.

SHEILA: I want to be married and have kids. With the right man. Someone who's ready to settle down. It must be lovely to be in love.

They are silent.

Nils. Most guys can't wait to jump on me.

NILS: What?

SHEILA: So are you going to ask me out on a date or not?

NILS: No. Yes.

From the living room.

AUNTY: I think it's the beginning of a deep and meaningful relationship.

MADHU: I will be happy. And my Nils will be happy too.

INDIRA: It'll be the wedding of the year.

Scene 6

The hijra home, that evening.

The GURU HIJRA, wearing a brightly coloured silk sari and decorated with gold and diamonds, watches the HIJRA do a ritual to Lord Rama. An adorned life-size statue of the Hindu god Rama stands beside where the GURU HIJRA is sitting. NILS enters and the GURU HIJRA acknowledges him and beckons him to be seated on a floor cushion. The prayer comes to an end.

GURU: Jolly good my dear. Here this is for you.

She hands her a present but the HIJRA is more interested in NILS.

Look how you affect her Nils with your beauty. You have more than one admirer in this house. Welcome to my home. Offer him some sweets and a drink. What would you like?

NILS: Anything.

GURU: (*Whispering.*) Have a watercolour drink, gin and tonic. We don't like to drink too obviously in front of Lord Rama on his birthday. It's not very polite. Go and ask Rani to bring us some watercolour. She mixes a smashing G&T.

NILS: Thank you. I need it.

The GURU HIJRA is amused.

GURU: We're pleased you could join us on this auspicious day.

NILS: Where is Raj?

GURU: He's just coming. He's told me a lot about you.

NILS: I hope it is all good.

GURU: Why, shouldn't it be?

NILS: No... No.

GURU: I'm only teasing you.

The HIJRA and RAJ, dressed as a woman, enter. He gives the GURU HIJRA and NILS their drinks and some savoury snacks. NILS does not recognize RAJ. He sits in the corner. NILS offers the GURU HIJRA some snacks.

No thank you. I am fasting today. Entertain us.

She takes a swig of her drink. The music starts again. RAJ and the HIJRA start to dance.

Has Raj told you the story of Lord Rama and us?

NILS: No.

GURU: The dance tells the story.

She pauses to watch the dance.

Centuries and centuries ago during the era of Satyug when the gods walked the earth, the great Lord Rama was forced into the jungle. Do you know the story of this epic?

NILS: Yeah, I saw it on the box, on TV, eh um on telly. In London, when they showed *The Mahabharata.*

GURU: No silly boy, *The Ramayana.* Well they never told our story, it is one of many great injustices we have suffered. But god himself saved us. You see we were rewarded for our loyalty, but Hindus throughout the World refuse to accept it. There was great sadness that day Lord Rama was exiled. The news quickly spread and villagers from miles and miles around followed. Millions and millions of crying people.

RAJ and the HIJRA continue to dance.

Lord Rama told the people to go home. But nobody moved away, 'I demand that you leave, forget me. I order it. Honour your new king'. And he disappeared into the jungle with his wife, Sita, and devoted brother.

NILS: But how do you fit into the story?

GURU: After fourteen long and hard years they returned and found us living at the edge of the forest. 'Why are you still here?' Lord Rama shouted, 'How dare you disobey me!' But my ancestor the great Gurumaa, may her name be blessed, challenged our Lord, she challenged God himself asking that such an insult should be withdrawn 'You demanded that all men and women should return to their homes, but we are the third gender, neither man nor woman'. Lord Rama was so moved by our loyalty that he granted us the power of the third eye to grant wishes and cast spells.

NILS: That's why you're given money?

GURU: Hindus fear that they may anger us. And we have the power over life and death.

NILS: So are there a lot of...eh...you lot around then.

GURU: Hundreds of thousands of us in India alone. We will not be forgotten. This is our revenge, our united strength only reminds the world of it weakness and intolerance.

The dance comes to an end.

So you wish to take my son away from me.

NILS: I...

GURU: I am pleased for him and you of course. But now we have to find a way for you both to be together. I understand you wish to return to England quite soon.

NILS: Yes. I have to.

GURU: It is so rare to meet someone with whom one falls in love in this life, and so it is always worth a great fight to keep that love once it has been found. You do love my son?

NILS: It's difficult. I live there, he lives here.

GURU: Ahhh. We have a plan. Rani.

RAJ rises.

RAJ: Hello Nils. I'm going to be your wife, Rani.

NILS: What?

GURU: I've got Raj a false passport and medical certificate.

RAJ: I can come to London.

NILS: What?

GURU: Everything will be okay. You can be together.

NILS: What?

RAJ: Can't you say something else?

NILS: Gosh.

GURU: It's the only solution.

NILS: Yes... I mean oh my God.

RAJ: What is it Nils?

NILS: What?

RAJ: Now Nils. What are you thinking? What is it?

NILS: Gosh.

GURU/RAJ: Nils!

Scene 7

Airport. Day.

MADHU is waiting with loads of luggage ready to go back to Nairobi.

ANNOUNCER: Can Mr. Henry Singh Sahota travelling to Nairobi on Air India Flight zero, zero, two please meet his mother at the meeting point.

NILS enters.

NILS: I had to bribe the bloke with a hundred rupees just so I could enter the airport. Security, he said.

MADHU: Where's aunty?

NILS: She refused to pay the money. I offered but she said no. She's still negotiating.

ANNOUNCER: Henry Singh Sahota, your mother has bought you some roti and sabzi and it is getting cold. Please meet her at the meeting point.

NILS: You must be pleased you're going home to Nairobi after all this time in India.

MADHU: I wish you would come and live with us. I do miss you.

NILS: I'll come to Kenya for the summer.

MADHU: (*Half laughing.*) You're the worst boy anyone could hope for.

ANNOUNCER: Henry. Henry go to the meeting point now, jaldi, jaldi. Your mother has been cooking for you all afternoon, is this the way to treat her?

MADHU: So have you made a decision about Sheila?

NILS: The sale of the century...

MADHU: I hear you're meeting her later.

NILS: Don't go jumping to any conclusions. I was badgered into it.

MADHU: What is wrong with her? She's one of our own so she'll easily adapt to our family. She's beautiful, educated, good...

NILS: Oh, Mum, stop going on. Why do you always have to stick your nose into my business?

ANNOUNCER: Henry! Henrryyyyy!

NILS: I am not marrying Sheila or anyone else. Understand! End of story.

MADHU: Alright. Alright. But why? (*Laughing.*) Are you a pervert? Is that what it is? Don't tell me you're a pervert.

NILS: Mum, I'm going.

MADHU: Don't be like that. I'm your mother. I was only joking.

NILS: You two got together and made my life hell. Always arguing, you were useless parents both of you.

They are silent.

MADHU: That's not fair. I had no say in anything, not with your father. One word and I'd get a slap.

NILS: You should have left him.

MADHU: Where else was I meant to go, and you still at school. I had to stick with him. I had no money, I had nothing, no friends, no social life without him. I was stuck. I never wanted you to be unhappy. I tried so hard to keep you out of it. I always thought that one-day when you got married things would be better. Maybe they will be when you are settled.

They are silent.

NILS: Mum, I don't want to let you down. I have something to tell you.

MADHU: You're a good boy. My favourite boy. You are all I've got. I just don't want you to make the same mistakes we made. Whatever you do that makes you happy will make me happy too. Just make the right decision.

NILS: Mum…

MADHU: But I think Sheila is a lovely girl. You couldn't find anyone better, Please Nils. Flirt with her. Show her a good time. Woo her.

NILS: Mum it's time for you to go. Come on.

Scene 8

Chowpati Beach. Night.

RAJ: Who's Sheila?

NILS: Oh she's a friend of the family. Like my sister. Actually she's a girl they're trying to set me up with.

RAJ: I see.

Silence.

This is where we met. Remember. Over there by the pani puri stall. You were outrageous and flirted with me. You called it Chapatti Beach even then.

NILS: You flirted back.

RAJ: Guess what? Everything's arranged.

NILS: Is it?

RAJ: Haan. Maa managed everything super quickly.

NILS is silent.

You don't seem very happy. Isn't this what we wanted?

NILS: Yes. But…

RAJ: What?

NILS: Do we really know what we're doing?

RAJ: It'll be fine, we'll pull it off. What's wrong Nils?

NILS: Raj, I'm not as courageous as you. I wish I was but I'm not.

RAJ: I know it'll be difficult but we have to try if we want to be together. Together Nils. We'll have each other. There's a ritual tomorrow. For us.

NILS: What's happening?

RAJ: It's our wedding day.

NILS: Our wedding day?

RAJ: Yes, we're getting married. My maa insists we do things properly. It's a hijra thing. She says I have to…

NILS: (*Laughing.*) Get married someday and be settled.

RAJ: Yes. Anyway we need a marriage certificate for my visa.

NILS: You're crazy. As mad as tits.

RAJ: It's romantic.

NILS: You're mad.

SHEILA sits on the beach. She spots NILS and waves.

There's Sheila. I've got to go.

RAJ: So will I see you tomorrow at noon?

NILS: Yeah.

They are silent.

RAJ: I guess I'd better go then.

Silence.

Bye.

He leaves.

SHEILA: Nils, hi.

NILS: Hi.

He walks over to her.

SHEILA: Who was that man you were talking to?

NILS: Oh. A friend, just a friend. So you alright?

SHEILA: Yes. Great. I'm glad you phoned me. I was hoping you would.

NILS: Sheila, we need to talk. It's important.

He sits down.

SHEILA: Good. Let's talk.

They are silent.

I love it here. It's so peaceful.

NILS: I come here sometimes to get away.

SHEILA: I know exactly what you mean. Mothers! India!

NILS: Yours gives you a hard time sometimes, doesn't she?

SHEILA: I get used to it.

NILS: Used to it or you just put up with it?

(*SHEILA is silent.*)

NILS: We're similar you and I. Children of controlling parents.

SHEILA: I saw that show too. On Oprah wasn't it.

NILS: (*US accent.*) Thank God for Ms Winfrey. What would we screwed-up beings do without her?

SHEILA: Have more damaged kids. So what did you want to talk about?

NILS: Nothing.

SHEILA: Go on. Don't be shy.

(*NILS is silent.*)

SHEILA: Whenever I have problems I make a decision and just act on it and not think of the consequences. It usually solves the problem.

NILS: If only it were so simple.

SHEILA: Sometimes they're easier to solve than you think. It's all about trusting yourself. Being courageous.

NILS: Thanks, therapist.

SHEILA: Are you laughing at me?

NILS: No, Sheila, I'm not. I wouldn't do that. Honest. I like you. You're a wright you are.

SHEILA: Am I?

NILS: Yeah. Stop being so hard on yourself.

SHEILA: Nils, you're very kind. You make me feel exuberant.

She kisses him and he slowly kisses back.

People are watching.

She kisses him again.

I was hoping this was going to happen.

NILS: Sheila, I'm sorry. We shouldn't do this. I can't.

He stands up.

SHEILA: Where are you going?

NILS: I've got to go. I'm sorry.

He runs off.

SHEILA: Got him.

Scene 9

The hijra home. Day.

A shinai is heard and the HIJRA dances whilst the GURU HIJRA sits under a mandap (Wedding canopy) in front of the wedding fire. RAJ enters tied to NILS with the marriage knot. They circle the fire three times and sit as the GURU HIJRA recites Sanskrit prayer verses and pours rice and ghee on the fire.

RAJ: I thought we'd be fighting over who'd wear the mehndi.

NILS and RAJ laugh. The GURU HIJRA blesses the bride and groom by placing red powder, followed by rice on their foreheads. The HIJRA continues to dance as the GURU HIJRA rises.

I'll follow you in a few weeks, as soon as you send me the sponsorship papers so I can get my visa. Sort it out quickly. I can't bear to be away from you.

NILS: I'm sure it's not going to work. It'll never work.

GURU: Trust in the universe. It has a strange force. And we have the power of Bahucharu Maa with us. She'll protect you.

The boys bow down and touch her feet.

Today you have initiated a process within you and that journey will cause conflict but see that pain as a gift and the road to empathy and tolerance. Remember the link between Heaven and Earth begins and ends within you. That energy is precious and should be treated with the utmost respect. It is the way to discover the secret of life and ultimate happiness. (*To RAJ.*) I shall miss you but I'll be watching over you.

RAJ: Oh maa.

GURU: (*To NILS.*) Look after my Raj.

NILS: I will. But this will never work.

RAJ: Want a bet?

> *The HIJRA brings out a burkha and puts it over RAJ so that only his eyes are visible. They hug. The shinai plays as the sound of an aeroplane is heard. The GURU HIJRA and the HIJRA wave towards the sky.*

> *End of Act One.*

ACT TWO

Scene 1

The Mehta's home, Wembley, England. Day.

Suitcases stand by the door. NILS stands alone.

NILS: Come on quickly, before anyone sees us.

RANI: (*Off-stage.*) It's a tradition to carry the new bride over the threshold.

NILS: Get a life!

He carries RAJ/RANI dressed in a red wedding sari, on stage.

RANI: Baby we did it. I missed you madly. The last few weeks have been agony. But now we're together. At last.

NILS: We did it. I can't believe it. I need a drink.

RANI: Champagne? I bought it duty free. Yes champagne. It's made in India.

He gives NILS a bottle of champagne.

NILS: There's a lot to plan.

RANI: What right now? Cool it. We'll do it tomorrow. I'm bushed after that flight.

He lounges on the sofa as NILS gets two champagne flutes.

Nils, I can't see the difference between here and India. I haven't seen one white face yet.

NILS: The people who live at number fourteen are English. Now first things first.

He opens the bottle of champagne and pours.

RANI: To us, mister and mister and missus Nils, Raj and Rani Mehta.

They both drink.

Cheers. We should remember this moment. It's one of those special times at a turning point in our lives. I can't remember any more what life was like before I met you. I want everyone to see how happy I am.

NILS: Raj I'm really glad to see you but…we have to be careful.

RANI: I know.

NILS goes over to RAJ and takes his wig off.

NILS: I'll say you're a friend of mine from India and that you've come over here to study.

RANI: Okay yaar.

NILS: We will have to create a background story for you.

RANI: Yes sir.

NILS: We all have to recreate ourselves sometimes. A new wife doesn't only change her name, she has to change her life too.

RANI: Very funny. Give me a kiss.

The bell rings.

NILS: Quick. Raj. Get your kit off.

RANI: What! Do you know how long it took to get this all on?

NILS: Hide.

RANI: Where?

NILS: Upstairs.

RANI: Okay.

NILS: Hurry!

RANI: All right. Calm down.

He exits. NILS opens the front door and BOBBY walks in.

NILS: Hey, Bobby.

BOBBY looks around the room.

BOBBY: Who's that woman you were with?

NILS: What woman?

BOBBY: The bird in the sari. I saw your car pulling up. She looked horny. Is she shagable?

NILS: I got married.

BOBBY: You what?

NILS: You heard.

BOBBY: Married married?

NILS: Yes, in India.

BOBBY: I'm your mate and your solicitor, so how come I don't know anything about this?

NILS: It just happened. In Bombay.

BOBBY: (*Whispering.*) Where is she?

NILS: Upstairs.

BOBBY: Well. You gonna let me see your bird then?

NILS: Rani, oh Rani. Darling. Come on down. Rani baby.

BOBBY: Have you told her? You know, that you're a pillow biter?

NILS: Don't say that. It's not very funny. Jerk.

BOBBY: Sorry, shirtlifter. But does she know?

NILS: What d'you think?

BOBBY: What about all that you couldn't do that to a woman stuff? And you couldn't live a lie? But will you be able to do the (*Jamaican accent.*) bizness?

RAJ enters.

NILS: Rani, this is my best mate Bobby. This is Rani.

RAJ does a namaste.

BOBBY: Hello. Nice to meet you.

He puts his hands together in a namaste gesture.

(*To NILS.*) Does she speak English? (*To RAJ.*) Sorry my Gujarati is not very good.

NILS: She's Punjabi.

BOBBY: That doesn't help.

RANI: I know English.

BOBBY: So you managed to hook old bachelor boy. Well done. For marriage. Good.

NILS: It'll be your turn next.

BOBBY: Some chance of that. Rani you know anyone for me in India? Girl for me?

RANI: There are lots of girls in India.

BOBBY: I don't want a modern one. No modern. I want traditional girl. I prefer the traditional type, if you know what I mean. Like you. I'm not saying you're not modern. I mean… I don't know what I'm saying.

RANI: You mean a slave.

BOBBY: No! Leave it out. What d'you think I am?

NILS: He'd be happy with anyone who'd have him. Rani will you get another glass?

RANI: Champagne, Bobby?

BOBBY: Yeah. (*Whispering to NILS.*) I need it, the shock mate. So you shagged her yet? Cor! Big tits.

NILS: Watch what you say. You're talking about my wife mate.

BOBBY: Sorry. She's awright. Sexy, real horny. I like birds in their saris.

NILS: Hands off she's mine. Find your own.

BOBBY: She must know lots of new totty in India. Yes. So why'd you do it mate?

NILS: I fell in love.

BOBBY: Ask her if she's got a mate.

As RAJ hands BOBBY the glass, he takes off the wig. NILS and RAJ laugh.

Bugger me!

NILS: Bobby, this is Raj.

RANI: Hello Bobby. So I convinced you.

BOBBY: Course you didn't. I knew. I was just having you on.

NILS: Yeah right!

BOBBY: Why did you do it?

RANI: Because we love each other.

NILS: We beat immigration. Manipulated the system.

BOBBY: How?

NILS: Got a false passport mate.

BOBBY: You jammy buggers. Or should that be buggerers.

NILS: All right Bobby that's enough!

BOBBY: Joke. So what are you going to do now?

NILS: We're going to say Raj is a friend of mine from Bombay. We've worked it all out.

BOBBY: But you can't.

NILS: Why not?

BOBBY: What about immigration?

NILS: It'll be okay. He's in now.

BOBBY: But what about spot checks?

NILS/RANI: Eh?

BOBBY: They could, if they wanted to, check any time. Raj you have to stay as a girl until your immigration papers are sorted out.

RANI: Does that mean I have to stay like this?

BOBBY: Yes. You can't risk it.

RANI: How long for?

BOBBY: Usually two years.

RANI: Two whole years!

BOBBY: Maybe even longer.

RANI: Longer!

BOBBY: You may be able to get it down to eighteen months.

RANI: Eighteen months! Nils!

NILS: But I can't just move in with a woman Bobby. What will everyone say? You know what it's like here in gujuland mate. A bunch of chinwaggers.

BOBBY: That's why Rani has to keep to wearing a sari and you'll have to keep to your story and say you're married. If immigration get suspicious and they start snooping they may ask people.

RANI: Your wife! Nils!

NILS: Well I can't say you're a boy dressed in drag, can I? Christ!

RANI: Why can't we go away?

BOBBY: Whatever you do, you'll have to be on your guard. If you'd stayed together in India for two years, Raj would have been given leave to stay in the UK.

RANI: What! You idiot Nils!

NILS: We'll sort it out Raj.

RANI: When?

NILS: Well don't blame me. After all this was yours and your mother's idea originally.

RANI: I'm going to change.

NILS: Stay in a sari though.

RAJ exits.

(*Calling after.*) Raj, it'll work out. Trust me. Shit!

BOBBY laughs.

BOBBY: Well, that's another fine mess you've got me into.

NILS: Shut up.

BOBBY: Look you convinced me. I'm sure you could convince everyone else. And it would sort out all your problems if you had a wife.

He laughs.

NILS: Shut up. Just shut up.

BOBBY: Awright! Awright! Prissy little queen.

Scene 2

MRS PATEL's shop. The next day.

INDIRA: Mrs Patel, India was great. I did lots of shopping, bought everything. But what's the point of me having so much money if I'm not going to spend, spend, spend on me, me, me. *Hai ne* Mrs Patel? And then there's...

MRS PATEL: So much shopping to do and not enough time. So much to buy and not enough money. God is so cruel to us poor people. And with my daughter's wedding coming up so soon.

INDIRA: Yes, it's best to have a small wedding. So much cheaper.

MRS PATEL: Are you saying I'm stingy or something? I can afford to have the best for my daughter. I've invited one thousand people and I've hired the Copeland School. What to do? I can't just not invite people. Hai ne Indira?

INDIRA: And what a boy she's marrying. So ordinary.

MRS PATEL: At least my daughter could find a husband. How's your Sheila? Poor thing.

INDIRA: Very well. She's engaged.

MRS PATEL: Ohhhhhh! Why didn't you tell me sooner? Finally she managed. To who?

INDIRA: To a very good boy. Mrs Patel, you'll never guess whom to.

MRS PATEL: No I never will. Tell me.

INDIRA: Nils Mehta.

MRS PATEL: Hai Ram!

INDIRA: It was agreed in Bombay. They're going to get married later this year. Small wedding, just three thousand people at the Hilton Hotel. What to do?

MRS PATEL: You are talking about Madhu's Nils, no?

INDIRA: My dear darling, there's only one Nils Mehta worth taking to or about.

MRS PATEL: Oh yes, there's a lot to talk about, my dear madam. Oh you're going to get your chadi in a twist over this one.

INDIRA: What is it? What's happened?

MRS PATEL: I'm not one to gossip but I saw him, with these very eyes. Only yesterday. Going into his house with a girl and she's stayed put ever since.

INDIRA: You must be mistaken. He's promised to my Sheila.

MRS PATEL: I'm not blind you know.

INDIRA: It must be a relative of his.

MRS PATEL gets out a pair of binoculars and looks through them.

MRS PATEL: That is no relative. I saw her kissing. (*Whispering.*) They were doing the deep throat kissing, init!

INDIRA: Chi chi!

MRS PATEL: And they slept in the same room, together, all night long. It looked like naked.

INDIRA: Chi chi chi!

She grabs the binoculars and peers through them.

I can't see anything.

MRS PATEL: All's quiet on the Mehta front now. But later, after dark, he's doing the jiggi jiggi with a stranger init.

INDIRA: Chi chi chi chi chi chiiiiiiiiii.

MRS PATEL: Poor Sheila.

INDIRA: I've even announced the engagement.

MRS PATEL: Who will marry her now? Another breakdown. How many broken engagements has she had? Poor thing. Her reputation is ruined.

INDIRA storms out as MRS PATEL picks up her mobile phone.

MRS PATEL: Blahblahbahen…

Scene 3

The Mehta home. Next day.

NILS watches football on television.

NILS: Yes. What a moron. Come on. Yes, yeah.

RAJ enters wearing Punjabi dress.

Yeahhhhhhhhh! Goal. Raj we scored. Two nil up. I tell you the boy's a genius.

RAJ switches off the TV.

What you doing?

RANI: We have to talk.

NILS: It'll be over soon. Come and watch.

RANI: I want to go out.

NILS: No! You can't.

RANI: Nils!

NILS: Alright, alright. I've thought about it. It's gonna be okay. Let's talk. You look sexy in your sari.

RANI: Nils! What are we going to do?

NILS: I'll tell my parents I want to live closer to my new job.

RANI: What about immigration?

NILS: I'll buy a flat in town somewhere. If we keep to ourselves we'll be okay. English people won't even notice us. They're like that. And if anyone comes to check we'll say you're out.

He smiles.

RANI: Whatever happened to parties and a house in the country?

NILS: I didn't imagine it'd be like this. Do you wish you'd stayed in India?

RANI: No. I want to be with you. I love you.

NILS: When we go away, we'll have a fresh start.

RANI: That's all I want. Peace.

NILS: Ahhhh.

They kiss and hug as the sound of a key trying to open the front door is heard.

What's that?

RANI: What?

NILS: That.

MADHU walks in.

Mum!

MADHU: Hello darling.

NILS: What are you doing here?

MADHU: I got the first flight here as soon as I heard. I didn't even tell your father. What is going on here? Nils?

RANI: Hello, erm, Mum.

MADHU: It can't be true. Who is this Nils?

NILS: This is Rani, my wife.

MADHU: From where? Come on Nils.

NILS: Err…

MADHU: What sort of joke are you playing? Who is she?

NILS: Um…

MADHU: Where did she come from? Chor bazaar?

NILS: It happened in Bombay.

MADHU: Why didn't you tell me? Why the secrecy?

RANI: It was my fault. I persuaded him. Don't get angry with him.

MADHU: You may have married my son, but I'm still his mother.

NILS: You had your heart set on Sheila.

MADHU: Imagine how I felt, getting a phone call out of the blue from Mrs Patel of all people…

NILS: Mrs Patel!

RANI: Please don't be angry. I was looking forward to meeting you.

MADHU: I'm not angry. It's just so unexpected. I'm surprised he's married. I thought he never would. Is it because you're not Gujarati that Nils didn't tell me?

NILS: Yes.

RANI: No.

MADHU: Oh.

The bell rings urgently.

Who can that be?

INDIRA barges in.

MADHU: Indira.

INDIRA: What is going on here? (*To NILS.*) You have no shame.

She spots RAJ.

Look at that face. Look at that face! It's the kind of face only her mother could love. Madhu, poor you. The shame of it, you must feel so embarrassed. You don't know anything about her. Such a shock! Your own son doing such a thing to you behind your back.

She tuts.

MADHU: What's happened has happened.

INDIRA: You led us to believe that things were settled. We had even announced the engagement.

NILS: I'm sorry

INDIRA: (*To NILS.*) You can shut your face.

MADHU: What can I say? I was happy with him marrying Sheila. But what could I do?

INDIRA: No. You're only the mother. How long has it been going on for?

MADHU: Indira, I know you're upset but this is no way to act.

INDIRA: Then how do you expect me to react? Just sit back and take it like some sort of fool. You and I had an arrangement and you broke it. End of story.

MADHU: There has been no formal engagement so nothing is broken.

INDIRA: I have to put up with this humiliation. I have no choice, but your attitude that I cannot accept.

RANI: Well you have to. There's nothing you can do about it.

MADHU: Rani!

INDIRA walks up to RAJ and looks at him.

INDIRA: Don't you get cocky with me. Don't think anyone will want you here, my girl. I'm certain you don't live up to our standards. So I wouldn't get too comfortable. Ha! (*To NILS and MADHU.*) She lives up to expectation. What a family! Ha!

She exits and everyone is silent for a moment.

MADHU: Well thank God I won't have to put up with her any more. The stuck up cow.

RANI: Don't insult a cow.

MADHU: Such a silly woman.

RANI: (*To NILS.*) She could have been your mother in law. (*To MADHU.*) You must be tired after your flight. Let me get you some tea and something to eat. Are you hungry? I've made some lamb just now.

MADHU: No meat. I'm strictly vegetarian. One hundred per cent.

NILS: She made it specially for me, me being strictly non veg.

RANI: I'm vegetarian also. I've cooked aloo bhindi. We can eat that.

MADHU: First a nice cup of tea would be nice. Come on, I'll help you make masala chai. Nils take my bags upstairs, Rani and I are going to have a chat. I want to know everything about you. Where did you study? And what did you do…

They exit. NILS picks up the bags.

NILS: Mum, why've you got so much luggage?

Scene 4

Park bench. Same day.

SHEILA: That marriage will never last.

INDIRA: You should see her.

SHEILA: What sort of marriage is it he has? He doesn't even take her out in public.

INDIRA: Well there you have it. She is a nothing.

SHEILA is silent.

SHEILA: Why did he do it? I thought he was different. He seemed so genuine.

INDIRA: Now toughen up. Drop this good girl act. It's got us nowhere. Honestly Sheila, you should see her. That face!

SHEILA: You're making me feel worse.

INDIRA: Poor you, you must be so angry. You have to win him back. Use a woman's most powerful weapon.

SHEILA: The way to a man's heart is through his stomach.

INDIRA: No sweetheart. Seduce him. Sex. No man can resist the temptation of a beautiful woman's body. Married or not. Give up your virginity, for your future. My girl, just because I brought you up to be a perfect Indian girl don't think we can't discuss sex. I mean for a country such as India where it is never discussed they have a mighty high population.

SHEILA: They don't talk about it because they're too busy doing it.

INDIRA: Yes dear! Sex is your mantrap.

SHEILA: Do you think it will work? Will he want me back? Can I really do it do you think?

INDIRA: Girl you have to fight with all you have. This is an emergency. You can't just stand back and be discarded. You have to get him back.

SHEILA: I want him back. I still really like him. He's penetrated my whole body, made me feel alive. I do want to make love to him. I want him to smother me. Do you really think he's made a mistake. It's all the pressure. He must have been forced into marrying her. Poor him. He must be so unhappy. I can forgive him. I will.

INDIRA: Sheila! Have you no shame? Forgive him! We have to move on. You must become the other woman. When he's fallen for you, dump him.

SHEILA: Mum?

INDIRA: We can't let him get away with this. If I had let men treat me so badly, where would we be now? We have to get into action and get our revenge.

SHEILA: Stop it! Please!

INDIRA: He's humiliated me and you. Made us a laughing stock. Have you no pride in yourself my girl? He's ruined our reputation. Who will marry you now? What am I going to do now? It's hopeless. You must ruin his marriage.

SHEILA: Shut up! Shut up!

She lets out a loud piercing scream. There is silence.

INDIRA: Well! I'm only doing this for your own good. If you don't want my help, fine. We'll see how you manage then.

SHEILA: I'm better off without you. You don't care about how I feel. You never did!

INDIRA: Sheila, you're just upset. You don't mean it. You'll get over it and I'll find you a top boy. There's plenty more fish in the sea.

SHEILA gets up and exits.

Sheila, where are you going? Sheila?

Scene 5

The Mehta home. Day.

MRS PATEL, wearing a cardigan under her sari and Wellington boots, and MADHU drink tea. RAJ and NILS fold saris together. NILS is allergic to MRS PATEL's perfume and keeps sneezing loudly. RAJ keeps correcting his bosoms.

MRS PATEL: Lovely cup of tea.

MADHU: It's so nice of you to make the effort.

MRS PATEL: Our Nils has a wife, of course I wanted to meet her. Such a lovely girl she looks.

RANI: Thank you.

NILS: (*Whispering to RAJ.*) Be careful what you say. She's a double agent.

RANI: What is she wearing?

NILS: That perfume?

RANI: No, her clothes.

NILS: It's the fashion.

They laugh. NILS sneezes as RAJ corrects his bosoms.

MRS PATEL: What was that?

MADHU: Oh allergies.

MRS PATEL: Same old thing. I remember you when you were a little baby as if it were yesterday and always allergies and now look at you all grown up and married. Such a lovely girl. Rani please come to see me, an old woman working day and night. How we struggle in this country, I can't tell you. But what to do? *C'est la vie.* Yes come and see me.

RANI: I will.

MRS PATEL: Any time. Any time. I want to know everything about you. Why did you get married so quickly? You young people are so naughty. Everyone wants to know what has happened but I just tell them to mind their own. Nosy people init.

RANI: Yes they are.

NILS sneezes and RAJ corrects his bosoms.

NILS: (*Whispering.*) Why d'you keep doing that?

RANI: (*Whispering.*) They keep slipping.

NILS: (*Whispering.*) Your rags are sticking out of your blouse.

RAJ tucks them in.

MADHU: Are you okay?

RANI: Yes. Of course.

NILS sneezes and RAJ adjusts his bosom. NILS scowls.

MRS PATEL: Now Madhu, you will have to do some damage limitation. Have a puja and a party to celebrate the marriage, big party, show off party. Only the Hilton will do. After all we want Rani to be accepted in society. Rani, you're not pregnant are you? A bun underneath the bonnet init?

NILS sneezes and RAJ adjusts his bosom.

MADHU: Of course she's not.

MRS PATEL: Oh very good. You know what people say. Nothing better to do. Must go. But tell me what's what and I'll make sure we sort things out.

MADHU: Of course. Thank you for coming.

MRS PATEL: No problem. You're like my own family. Such a lovely girl.

She exits.

MADHU: Well at least we have her on our side.

RANI: Great! Now a party.

NILS: It's what everyone expects.

NILS sneezes again and RAJ sits down legs wide apart. NILS moves towards him, puts his hand on RAJ's knee and draws his legs together. RAJ crosses his legs and corrects his posture and his bosom. NILS sneezes. RAJ's bosom drops. NILS corrects it. MADHU sees, is shocked but ignores it.

MADHU: We have to do something. You know how nasty everyone can be. Rani, where do your parents live again?

RANI: Maa lives in Mumbai.

MADHU: I should phone her.

NILS: Mum! She's an orphan.

MADHU: Can't you two give me a straight answer for once. Rani after you've folded those saris the ones from yesterday all need to be ironed. You're getting behind. Nils you'd better help her. Oh.

She looks in her handbag and pulls out a tube.

You need this Rani. Immac for your legs. It's very good.

She hands it to RAJ as she exits. The boys are silent.

RANI: Do you think your mum has worked it out?

NILS: Of course not. We just have to carry on until she leaves.

RAJ is silent.

Mum likes you. You are so, so charming. See it wasn't that difficult.

RANI: I feel very bad about lying to your mother. How long will it have to go on for?

NILS: We didn't lie. We just didn't tell her the whole truth. We're pulling it off just fine.

RANI: We're going to be found out sometime or other. She wants to talk to my family. She'll want to invite them to the party.

NILS: It's your fault. I told you what to say.

RANI: Sorry I forgot.

NILS: Well be more careful. Raj we must keep this up. For us.

RANI: Bhus. Oh chup. It's easy for you.

They both fall silent as the music to 'Chalte Chalte' is heard softly. The GURU HIJRA enters, walks to RAJ and massages his forehead. She stops and steps back.

GURU: I told you I'd be with you. Tell Nils what you did today. Go on. It's okay.

RANI: I went out today. I put on my own clothes and
sneaked out. Don't worry nobody saw me. I went, as Raj,
to explore. I wanted to go on a tour alone in London. So
I was on the number eleven bus, the famous number
eleven, it goes from Fulham Broadway to Liverpool
Street. It's almost takes the same route as the tour bus
but much cheaper, over eight hundred rupees cheaper.
Of course, the upstairs of the bus was full of Indians,
they all know about it. There I was on my own, free,
seeing all the sights. St Paul's Cathedral, the River
Thames, the London Eye, Trafalgar Square.

And then two boys, about eighteen years old, entered
the bus and sat in the middle of the Indians oblivious to
anyone else. They were that type, you know who speak
the cockney language. Well one of the boys put his arm
around his friend. He was reading the newspaper and
when his boyfriend did it, he just continued to read.
It seemed as if it were the most natural thing to do and
it was.

And then he showed his friend something in the
newspaper and they were laughing and hugging, two
beautiful young men, madly in love. And nobody
noticed, everyone was too busy minding their own
business, in their own worlds. Then suddenly they started
kissing, real Frenchy style and only then did some
people point at them. Yes perhaps they were laughing at
them but others just ignored them. I have never seen two
boys show affection in public in such a way, never. I was
exhilarated but at the same time…envious, jealous of
their love, the fact they had each other, they didn't care
about anyone else. And then I thought about us and felt
sad and almost started to cry.

The GURU HIJRA massages him.

Because we will never be them, ever. If you were on that
bus with me you would have been laughing too.

They are silent.

We have to tell your mother the truth. Nils, don't you love me?

NILS: Well I wouldn't go through all this for nothing.

RANI: Then why is it so difficult for you?

NILS: What you and I have is private. Between us. We need to support each other to get through this. Both of us together. As soon as she leaves we'll go away. I promise.

RANI: Run away? I can hardly walk in this thing. I left everything, my home, my family and my country for us. What are you willing to give up Nils? Look at me Nils!

NILS: Why are you asking me to make a choice between my mother and you?

RANI: What would you do if I decide to throw off this sari. Eh? I refuse to live like this any more.

NILS: It's not my fault. I had no idea it was going to be like this.

RANI: We tell your mother. Or that's the end. We are finished. I go back.

NILS: Raj, be reasonable for Christ's sake.

RANI: No.

He exits followed by the GURU HIJRA. MADHU enters.

MADHU: What's all this shouting about? The whole street can hear you. Why are you arguing? What is Rani upset about?

NILS: It's nothing.

MADHU: What is wrong with you? You can't go around hurting people. It's wrong. First it was poor Sheila. You don't even seem to care about what you did to her. You broke a young girl's heart.

NILS: I'll sort it out with Sheila.

MADHU: And now Rani.

NILS: Why do you assume it's my fault?

MADHU: Because I know you.

NILS: Thanks for the support as usual mum.

MADHU: I know there is something wrong. Stop treating me as if I am stupid. Tell me the truth. What is going on? Nils, I want you to tell me.

NILS: It's your fault.

MADHU: Mine? What have I done now? Am I in the way?

NILS: No!

MADHU: You should have told me and I would have left. Tell me and I'll go. I can go back to Nairobi. Not that your father wants me anyhow.

NILS: Mum. Of course I don't want you to leave.

He puts his arm around MADHU.

I must talk to Rani.

MADHU: No. You both calm down a bit. I think it's about time I had a talk with Rani to straighten things out.

Scene 6

Bedroom. Same day.

RAJ packs his bags. The GURU HIJRA stands by him.

GURU: Raj, are you okay?

RANI: I want to come home.

GURU: You're just hurt. Wait and see what happens. Stay centred. Be patient.

MADHU enters.

MADHU: Rani, what are you doing? You're not leaving are you?

RANI: It's the best thing to do.

MADHU: I'd rather you stayed here.

RANI: No.

GURU: Patience.

MADHU: I know why you want to leave. But I want you to stay. I'm very fond of you.

GURU: You're always so headstrong. Listen to your heart. Be honest.

RANI: Ohhhh.

MADHU: Oh I see you're having a bad bosom day today.

RANI: Yes I need to go to Debenhams and buy some new silicone but Nils hasn't had the time to take me. I…

GURU: Not that honest.

RANI: Look what you made me do maa. How long have you known?

MADHU: So it is true.

RANI: Yes.

MADHU: Oh God! Are you sure?

They are silent.

Why did you do all this? All this show?

RANI: It was the only way we could be together.

MADHU: Why didn't you come over as a student?

RANI: I didn't have the money.

MADHU: Why didn't Nils tell me? I would have supported him. He's my son. I love him.

RANI: He was scared.

MADHU: How were you going to live like this? And now. What will everyone say? What a mess. I wanted him to get married but not to a boy with a bust made from rags.

She pulls out some of RAJ's padding. They are silent.

GURU: Tell her how you feel.

RANI: We did it because we love each other. And I couldn't bear to be away from him so it was my idea. I didn't want to be left alone. I'm sorry. I really am. We didn't want to hurt you, I promise. It's just…

They are silent. MADHU strokes RAJ's hair.

MADHU: Oh dear. What are you and Nils going to do?

RANI: I'll go home. It's the only way. Nils wants me to leave too.

MADHU: But he needs you. You two will work it out. It's just a silly fight.

GURU: Listen to what she is saying. Don't judge.

RANI: It's for the best. What else can I do?

MADHU: I know he wants you to stay.

RANI: No. I don't think so.

GURU: I do think so.

MADHU: You make him very happy.

RANI: Do I?

GURU: Of course.

MADHU: You can always tell by the quality of a man's orgasm.

RANI/GURU: Oh my god.

GURU: Hi, hi.

She exits.

MADHU: I've been married for over thirty years. As your mother-in-law it's my duty to teach you a thing or two about men. I can tell by the force of his sneeze. When a man is having good orgasms he is much more forceful with his sneezes. With vigour.

RANI: Oh Madhubahen.

He covers his face with his hands.

MADHU: Call me mum if you prefer. You're like my own child.

They hug.

Why didn't you say something, Rani?

MADHU: Because I didn't want it to be true. I thought he would be lonely and unhappy for the rest of his life.

RANI: He won't be. He has me.

MADHU: Yes. I know. He has a whole life I know nothing about. But now I'll have two sons to spoil me. I am so happy that Nils hasn't turned out to be like his father. So you are staying aren't you?

RANI: That's up to Nils.

MADHU: With your support, I think we can sort him out. You and I as a team. Go back to India and then come back on a student visa and then we'll marry him off to a lesbian. I read about it in Woman's Own. And don't worry how much it will cost. Do you like wearing saris?

RANI: No, but I've gotten used to them lately.

MADHU: But you have such good taste. We must go shopping together…eh?

RANI: Raj.

MADHU: Raj.

RANI: Oh Mum.

They laugh and hug again.

Scene 7

Bar.

SHEILA is sitting at a table in sexy and revealing clothes. An opened bottle of red wine and two glasses are on the table. SHEILA's is half empty. NILS runs in frazzled.

SHEILA: Hi.

NILS: Sorry I'm late.

SHEILA: I thought you weren't going to turn up.

NILS: I was delayed. Sorry.

SHEILA: Sit. Have a glass of wine.

She pours a glass for NILS and he drinks almost half of it in one go.

SHEILA: More?

She pours him more.

You nervous or something?

NILS: Why did you choose this bar? Lots of people I know come here.

SHEILA: Things aren't working out with Rani are they?

NILS: What?

SHEILA: It's okay. Everyone knows.

NILS: What's everyone saying?

SHEILA: Just gossip. You know you never take Rani out and stuff.

NILS is silent.

Thanks for agreeing to see me.

She lifts her glass.

SHEILA: Cheers. Friends.

NILS: Yes. Cheers. Yeah.

They are silent as they drink. SHEILA sips and NILS gulps and SHEILA pours him some more.

I feel better now.

SHEILA: Well you don't have to be scared of me. I'm just a pussycat.

NILS: I told you I'm not nervous.

SHEILA: I know. You've already said that.

NILS: I was really pleased when you phoned.

SHEILA: Were you?

NILS: Yes. You've been on my mind a lot. I'm sorry about what happened. Honestly. I'm sorry I hurt you.

SHEILA: We were both under a lot of pressure. So it's not surprising…mistakes are made!

NILS: You're right there.

SHEILA is silent.

SHEILA: What's wrong with you and Rani?

NILS is silent.

Why did you marry her, Nils?

NILS: It just happened.

SHEILA: Do you love her?

NILS is silent.

Why did you agree to meet me?

NILS: Until you called I thought you thought I was a jerk. But I always wanted us to be friends. I messed things up. I'm sorry.

SHEILA: Do you want us to try again? That's what you're saying aren't you?

NILS: No. Whoaaaaaaaaaaaaa!

SHEILA: Are you trying to say sorry?

NILS: Yes. You don't understand.

SHEILA: I do. I've been involved with the wrong people in the past too.

NILS: Please Sheila. I don't want to get involved like that with you.

SHEILA: Was I too pushy? Is that it?

NILS: No. Sheila, I'm sorry. It's my fault. Look you'll meet someone better than me.

SHEILA: I don't understand men. What is wrong with you all? Do you enjoy playing games? Do you get a kick out of hurting people? Everyone's saying I've had two broken engagements. Look at her, alone at her age. Poor thing! That's what they all say, I know. I want to be free from it all.

NILS: Sheila, you can't be free if you're scared of what everyone's saying.

SHEILA: What choice do I have? I'm stuck. And you're part of the problem. You put me in this position. What is wrong with me?

NILS: Look Sheila it has nothing to do with you. I'm gay.

SHEILA: Yeah right! Now you're going to tell me you like men. You like men more than you like me. And why did you lead me on so much? You kissed me. I thought we had something special.

NILS: I just did what I had to do.

SHEILA: Why are you being so cruel?

NILS: I'm sorry Sheila that was unfair of me. But it's true. I am gay. I could've married you and lied. But I didn't. I did the right thing for both of us.

SHEILA: Who the hell is Rani then?

She laughs.

NILS: That's a bloke.

She laughs more and then gets angry as BOBBY enters.

SHEILA: You bastard. You're just like the rest.

NILS: I'm sorry Sheila.

He leaves.

BOBBY: Heh, I'm Dr Bob, sex doctor.

SHEILA starts to cry.

Sheila, don't cry. What's wrong?

He takes out a handkerchief from his pocket.

Here wipe your eyes. Please don't cry.

SHEILA: Leave me alone.

BOBBY: What is it, Sheila? Tell me. I'm different. I'm a new man. Honest.

Scene 8

NILS' home, living room.

NILS enters. RAJ is sitting reading a book. The GURU HIJRA is reading a book called 'How to be Happy Homos'.

RANI: Nils that's brilliant.

NILS: Yep, I just blurted it out.

RANI: I'll give my saris to your mum as a present.

NILS: Don't say anything to her yet.

RANI: She already knows.

NILS: What!

RANI: I didn't have to say anything. She already knew.

NILS: How?

The GURU HIJRA sneezes.

RANI: She said you were very forceful with your sneezes.

GURU: With vigour.

NILS: What are you going on about?

RANI: It was obvious she said. In fact she suggested that I go back to India and then I come back as Raj and we live together here as a couple.

NILS: I don't believe she said that.

RANI: Well, she did.

NILS: And what will everyone else say?

RANI: Nils, you told Sheila. That means every Tom, Jit and sari will know in no time. You may as well have put an ad in the Wembley Gazette or the Gujarat Samachar.

NILS: Raj please. This is hard for me.

RANI: Sorry.

NILS: We're going to have to smarten you up. You'll have to enrol in college. How about Law?

RANI: I don't want to do Law. It's boring.

NILS: Well you've got to do something. What's wrong with law, it's a good job. What about accountancy? Or computing?

RANI: What has this got to do with us?

NILS: You've got to do something. You need a career.

GURU: How about a drag queen?

RANI: What would you say if I said I wanted to be a hairdresser?

NILS: What do you want to do that for?

RANI: An air steward?

NILS: Raj you can't tell everyone you're a trolley dolly.

RANI: Will you be embarrassed?

NILS: Everyone might accept us if we both are successful, sober and respectable.

RANI: Nils, to some we'll always be dogs. We should forget about what people think of us.

NILS: I want us to be normal blokes with normal lives. What's wrong with that? Can't you see? It'll help us fit in more.

RANI: Fit in! You don't understand, do you?

GURU: You'll never be happy homos.

RANI: How can we be together if you want to control my life and tell me how to act and what to do? I want an equal relationship, where I can be whoever I want to be. It will be my choice. What's the point otherwise Nils?

GURU: Bravo.

NILS exits.

RANI: What should I do, maa?

GURU: Be patient. I have a plan and I now loan you a gift.

RANI: What gift?

GURU: When it is time, you will ask for it my son. You will see.

She claps her hands and beckons towards the front door, and the doorbell starts to ring urgently. NILS and MADHU enter as RAJ exits, smiling. MADHU opens the door and MRS PATEL and INDIRA storm in.

INDIRA: This will not do at all.

MRS PATEL: All this parading about.

INDIRA: We do not approve.

MRS PATEL: This is a respectable community.

INDIRA: Bringing over a...homo!

MRS PATEL: To our own backyard.

The music to the song 'Chalte, Chalte' from the film 'Pakeezah' is heard. RAJ enters.

INDIRA/PATEL: Chi, chi, chi.

RANI: May I?

The GURU HIJRA signals her approval.

INDIRA: And to think you wanted your son to marry my Sheila. We have never heard of such behaviour.

MRS PATEL: Never in all the years we have been living in this country.

INDIRA/PATEL: We are not happy.

INDIRA: He will have to go back.

MRS PATEL: Otherwise we will report it to immigration.

INDIRA/PATEL: This is a respectable community. We are respectable people. And we do not approve!

GURU: Lewd, crude and rude.

RAJ dances very erotically with much sexual innuendo.

NILS: What are you doing?

MRS PATEL: Ohhhhhhhhhhhhhh!

INDIRA: Ahhhhhhhhhhhhhhh!

MRS PATEL: Is it a hijra?

NILS: Stop, stop, stop you're making things worse.

MADHU: Oh shut your face Nils. Shape up or break up.

MRS PATEL: Hi Ram, she's a hijra.

INDIRA: Ooh, hijra.

MRS PATEL: She's casting a spell on us. Run away. Quickly.

INDIRA: Run, run. Quickly.

They scream and run away. RAJ and MADHU laugh and hug.

NILS: Oh my God, oh my God.

Scene 9

The sound of many phones is heard.

RANI: More and more hijra are coming out. England's full
   of them.

GURU: The whole world is full of us.

RANI: And I thought I'd sit about doing nothing. The
   trouble is, there are too many Asians in this country.
   Whatever business there is to do, they have already
   saturated it.

MADHU: Well we found a gap in the market. Our own
   Hijra agency.

She clicks her fingers and a huge sign 'Hijra-R-Us' is displayed.

When are we interviewing?

RANI: This afternoon. And we're being photographed for
   Hello magazine this morning and tomorrow we're on
   Richard and whoever's standing in for Judy this week.

The Mehta's home. Next day.

NILS enters.

NILS: Raj this has gone too far. Mum?

MADHU: Nils?

NILS: (*To RAJ.*) I think it's better if you go back to India
   and leave us to sort things out here.

They are all silent for a moment.

GURU: Tell him you're happy here Raj.

RANI: But I'm happy here, aren't I mum?

MADHU: Yes and I'm happy that you're here too. You and I make a great team.

GURU: Bravo.

NILS: Oh that's just great. Here I am trying to get us out of this mess and you two want to act like schoolgirls. Raj I think we should talk about this alone.

MADHU: You and your secrets Nils.

NILS: Come on. Stop playing around. This is serious.

MADHU: You should have told me first instead of blurting it out to everyone else.

NILS: Awright but it's not going to sort out itself. God!

MADHU: We are sorting it out. Change that attitude of yours and then everything will fall into pieces.

The doorbell rings.

Who can that be?

She looks through the window.

RANI: Into place, Mum.

NILS: It's Mrs Patel.

MADHU: Let her in.

The bell rings again.

Let her in then.

NILS lets MRS PATEL in. She carries mittai (Indian sweets) and a saffron coloured sari. Her hands are together reverently and her head is covered. She goes to RAJ and bows at his feet.

MRS PATEL: Jai shri Krishna. Sorry, sorry, sorry. Please forgive me. Sorry Raniji. I had no idea. What a blessing to have a hijra in your home, Madhu.

RANI: It's okay I forgive you.

MRS PATEL: Raniji, my daughter is getting married. Please will you come and bless the wedding.

GURU: Arreh! How rude.

RANI: This is a little unusual. I normally like to choose the weddings I wish to attend.

MRS PATEL: Forgive me for my rudeness. Please but I am a poor stupid old woman. I have come personally to extend my personal invitation to everyone in this home you protect.

RANI: Maa, what should I do?

MADHU: Well her diary is getting very full. I will consider your proposal and inform you of our decision. But you must understand Raniji honouring you with her presence is very inconvenient to her. All engagements interfere with her routines.

MRS PATEL: Please except this mittai and gift as a will of good gesture.

MADHU takes it.

And of course a further offering will be made at the wedding.

GURU: Oh!

MADHU: You are too generous. Thank you. Goodbye.

She puts her hands together, bows slightly and leaves. NILS enters.

NILS: Raj, can we talk? Please.

RANI: I have a gap in my diary, let me see, between six and half past tomorrow evening. No, no I have to open a new Asian supermarket at that time, and then there's dinner with the High Commissioner. And then I'm a judge at the final of Mister Gay UK. Thursday? We can do lunch.

NILS: Don't do me any favours.

RANI: Oh darling, don't be like that. I was going to treat you and take you to your favourite restaurant.

He storms off.

MADHU: Good. That's it. Very good. Let him fight to get you.

GURU: He'll come around soon.

RANI: Do you think I'm being too hard on him?

GURU: Patience, my son.

Scene 10

The Mehta's home. Day.

NILS sits drinking beer whilst BOBBY and SHEILA smoke a joint.

BOBBY: Don't hog it Sheila. Etiquette remember.

SHEILA: Fag?

She offers her huge joint to NILS who ignores her. BOBBY and SHEILA laugh.

BOBBY: Nils it's a joke. Cheer up mate. Here.

NILS takes the joint.

Big init. Thought you'd like that. Who said size doesn't matter. Eh? Sheila rolled it. Be careful with that. It's pure skunk, no tobacco shit.

NILS hands BOBBY the joint.

The best mate. We want you to be the first to know. We are getting engaged. We're having an arranged marriage. And we are in love. This is the real thing, not like that bimbo before.

SHEILA: Love! It's being practical. We fulfil each other's needs. I'm beautiful and he's got good prospects.

BOBBY: Yes, my little bharfi.

SHEILA: My little gulab jamun.

BOBBY: Brown balls, init.

SHEILA and BOBBY laugh.

SHEILA: Cheer up, it's Diwali.

NILS: Yeah, right.

BOBBY hands SHEILA the joint.

BOBBY: They don't know whether to treat you as a saint or a sinner. What with the money you're raking in, a live hijra and all that auspicious stuff. Rich and famous.

SHEILA: A real hijra.

BOBBY: Come out later, Nils, it'll cheer you up. You can't stay depressed like this forever.

NILS: Maybe.

BOBBY: Raj is coming. He's a right laugh. You two should patch it up.

SHEILA: I think it's a real shame. You're both so sweet together.

BOBBY: We'll go to a gay bar if you'd prefer. It'll be like the old days and then to a club.

SHEILA: Yeah, I want to go to a gay bar. Different in it.

BOBBY: Init, darling, init. As if it's all one word and half drop the t. Init.

SHEILA: Init.

BOBBY: Yeah that's it.

They kiss on the lips passionately.

Relationship's simple. It's all about compromise, mate.

SHEILA: And mutual respect.

BOBBY: Oh yeah. Look at us. You could have it too.

NILS: Yuck!

BOBBY and SHEILA laugh. BOBBY shows SHEILA he has an erection. She jumps up.

SHEILA: We've got to go to the puja Raniji's doing.

BOBBY: Oh, God, not the temple again. Give me some of that. It's the only way I can cope with that stuff.

He takes the joint.

SHEILA: Yes, darling. I always go on Diwali and we can't miss Raniji. Why don't you come with us, Nils?

NILS: What's the point?

SHEILA: You're going to have to make a grand gesture. That's what I would want. To prove how much you love him. Like *An Officer and a Gentleman*, that movie. Remember that?

BOBBY: Wicked film.

NILS: I know there's a problem but how to get around it?

BOBBY: Maybe that's the problem mate. You're trying to get around it instead of dealing with it head on. Here this will help you.

He pulls out a very huge joint.

Sometimes it's good to get out of it. It gives you more confidence mate. Relinquishing responsibility. Be easy on it. Good stuff this. Got to go. I'll call you. Later.

SHEILA: Later.

They move off.

BOBBY: Completely drop the t.

SHEILA: La'er.

NILS is left on his own again. He smokes the joint.

Scene 11

Temple. Day.

MRS PATEL, BOBBY, SHEILA and INDIRA do 'Raas', Gujarati folk dancing with sticks, as MADHU performs a puja to Rama. Gujarati religious folk songs are heard. RAJ and the GURU HIJRA stand at a distance.

GURU: Lewd, crude and rude works.

RANI: Yeah, survival of the fittest.

GURU: And are you happy?

RANI: I think so.

GURU: What about Nils?

Silence.

GURU: Don't be too hard on him. He's trying the best way he can. Sometimes what we see as a small gesture is huge to other people. You just have to learn to read a person.

RANI: Well, he should understand me. I prefer huge actions.

GURU: Still the fighter. The question you have to ask yourself is, are you happier with or without Nils. In gaining wealth and success you've forgotten yourself. And because I love you my son, I have been more lenient with you. Now is the time to give up the gift I have loaned you.

RANI: Today it will end. Welcome back Raj, just a plain old-fashioned gay boy.

They hug and RAJ joins the Raas. Suddenly a load scream is heard.

NILS: Oh shit!

Everyone stops dancing and there is silence through which we hear high heel shoes. NILS enters dressed in drag. He goes up to RAJ and holds out his hand.

Raj.

RANI: Nils.

They hug and kiss and then hold hands. MADHU hides her face with her hands.

MRS PATEL: Ohhhhhhhhhhhhhhhhh!

BOBBY: Mate, you should have shaved your arms and chest. It looks a bit gross. (*To SHEILA.*) He's off his trolley. Completely off his face. I warned him.

MRS PATEL: Ohhhhhhhhhhh! What is this?

INDIRA: Hi Ram. Who do they think they are?

NILS: We're lesbians.

He blows then all a kiss and they walk off stage. MRS PATEL takes out her mobile phone.

MRS PATEL: Blahblahbahen, lesbians che…

Scene 12

The Mehta's home, sitting room.

RAJ and NILS enter laughing. They flop down on the sofa and NILS pulls off his wig. The GURU HIJRA is already sitting reading her 'Happy Homos'.

RANI: Home sweet home.

NILS: The looks on their faces when we came walking down the road. I could have died.

RANI: You're not used to wearing high heels.

NILS: Who invented them?

RANI: (*Tenderly.*) Who's sari now?

NILS: (*Apprehensive.*) It's my chapatti and I'll cry if I want to. So you're talking to me now.

RANI: Can't resist it.

NILS: Shall we start again?

RANI: If we both agree. That's all we have. You've got nothing to hide any more. Simple wasn't it?

NILS: But I don't want you like that. It's just I like blokes. If I wanted a woman I would have got married.

RANI: Tonight was my last public appearance. I'll have to go back to India.

NILS: And will you come back?

RAJ stands up and hands NILS the end of his sari.

RANI: Here, pull.

NILS: What?

RANI: Pull.

NILS pulls the sari as it unfolds and ends up in his lap. RAJ then undresses out of the rest of his clothes to his boxer shorts and NILS does the same. They flop down on the sofa again.

Hello again. Hot isn't it?

NILS: Yeah, you're looking good.

RAJ: Didn't mean me.

NILS: Oh.

RAJ: I meant you.

NILS: Yeah?

RAJ: Hm, hm.

NILS: I want you to come back here to me.

RAJ: Yeah? You'll have to beg for it.

NILS: Woof, woof.

RAJ: Will you marry me?

NILS: I love you.

RAJ: They say the way to a man's heart is through his stomach.

NILS: Hm, hm.

RAJ: Go on then, drop your boxers.

GURU: Hii! Hii!

She throws her book in the air.

The End.